Hey, Darlin'

" Here on earth, tho', we still remember the past; we still blink into the future. There is no eternity other than the present which goes on forever. We come and we go. It is a lovely show."
                    Johar—

HEY DARLIN'
EPITAPHS FROM THE OREGON TERRITORY

JOHAN MATHIESEN

DeadManTalking
PORTLAND, OREGON

DEADMANTALKING
3044 SE 9th Avenue
Portland, OR 97202
johan.mathiesen@gmail.com

Book set in Palantino typeface; heads in Charlemagne Std.

All photographs by the author.

ISBN-13: 978-0615724225

TO MY CHILDREN
IN ORDER OF APPEARANCE

•

JANOS
LAVRANS
KEIRA
MATHIAS

TABLE OF CONTENTS

"LORD, THE TIMES WE HAD TOGETHER"

"The rarest thing in an epitaph is truth. "
Henry David Thoreau, quoted in
A Book of Epitaphs (1967) by Raymond Lamont Brown

EOPLE HAVE NEVER GONE GENTLY INTO THAT GOOD NIGHT; instead they're wont to erect a monument to themselves, standing as a beacon against the dying of the light. The Pyramids are a gross example, but they set the tone for all those unwilling to go quietly. Literacy provided another way of living beyond one's call of years. A good epitaph takes on a life of its own. Consider Rodney Dangerfield's "There goes the neighborhood." I suspect it will be funny long after they've forgotten who Rodney Dangerfield was.

As long as epitaphs have been chiseled into stone, people have been collecting them. They've collected them, largely, from two classes: humor or famous people. The same epitaphs, whether apocryphal or not, appear in collection after collection. The Internet rattles with them. Confusion reigns between which epitaphs actually got carved on a stone versus those which were just suggested, as, say, Hemingway's "Pardon me for not getting up." The two epitaph collections I was able to quickly unearth at my local library, Raymond Lamont Brown's *A Book of Epitaphs* (1967), and Nigel Rees's *Epitaphs: A Dictionary of Grave Epigrams and Memorial Eloquence* (1993), are classic examples of just

1

such collections. Both concentrate on particular types of epitaphs from, largely, particular classes of people. Both tend to lean towards English curiosities. Neither makes any pretense of using epitaphs as mirrors to everyday life (despite what Brown claims). The enormous, reflective category of quotes as epitaphs is entirely absent from either book.

Beyond those special groupings, epitaphs are largely ignored. Papers get occasionally written about the linguistic implications of certain wordings on tombstones in a handful of cemeteries in Croatia or the like; but scant attention is paid to what people—just average, everyday people—write on their tombstones. What your grandmother had written on her tombstone probably won't make it past Find-a-Grave. In going back over the table of contents for *Markers*, the journal of the Association for Gravestone Studies, for example, I only found five articles dealing with epitaphs at all; and only one of which, Gay Lynch's "Contemporary Gravemarkers of Youth: Milestones of Our Path through Pain and Joy," tried to look at general trends in contemporary usage. Let's just say there's a lot of room for research.

This particular project is anything but scientific; I have covered no ground thoroughly. Think of me more as a Darwin (yes, I like that comparison), off collecting examples of exotica. I didn't do counts. I can make no comparisons as to size, frequency, etc. Whole classes of epitaphs I largely ignored. "Gone fishing," for example, is nowhere in this collection (that's a lie). "Gone for the bait," on the other hand, is. Likewise I ignored countless *Bible* verses, including all the ones which were only book, chapter, and verse numbers. My curiosity didn't drive me to record or look them up. Shame on me; I might have missed some gems. And why someone would spend money to say "Gone but not forgotten" is beyond me. That's not an epitaph calculated to be remembered. So, what you have here is not representational of what's out there; what you have is what I determined to be of the most interest. Yes, me. Moi. No one else. This is where science gets thrown out the window. I can't give you any hard facts; all I can do is sketch the territory for you, give you an idea how far away is the horizon.

On the other hand, someone had to do this round before the next round of study could begin. We had to first know what was out there before we could decide where to look next. We had to get an idea of the scope of the resource. Hence, I spent the last eight years tramping around obscure and remote cemeteries dragging epitaphs from under the sage brush and moss. Thank God for the digital camera as I'd never have had the patience to hunker down and transcribe them all in the wind, cold, and weather.

The resulting 1100 epitaphs were extracted from better than 750 cemeteries, 630 or so from Oregon and the rest from Washington and Idaho with a scattering from elsewhere. This, perforce, means that any inferences drawn from their scrutiny can only be applied locally and it will take someone else looking at their neck of the woods to make valid comparisons; nonetheless, seeing what I do see on Flickr and my own experiences, what happens elsewhere in the country appears similar to what happens here. Our culture is, if not uniform, then at least inter-connected; what happens in Portland, Maine, is not so different from that which happens in Portland, Oregon. If you were an observer from Mongolia, it would all look pretty much the same, mountains and islets notwithstanding.

The first task was to divide the epitaphs into categories, which is where working in a survey research lab lo these many years ago came in han-dy. I've had experience making groups out of essays. The process was one of spreading the epitaphs out onto a large table, one-by-one, and making piles of ones that are similar. It doesn't take long for natural groups to appear from the formless mass. "Humor," indeed, was an obvious and early group, but "Famous People" fell by the wayside, un-less they had an interesting epitaph. Just being famous didn't qualify one for inclusion. I know Linus Pauling is out there, but his stone says nothing. Likewise Virgil Earp. Wit was sufficient to merit a place in the collection but not a necessity. I looked for any turn of phrase that caught my eye. In the end, ten or so categories came together depend-ing on how you're counting.

What I didn't do was divide them by who chose the epitaph; it's not always easy to tell: survivor or deceased? To a certain extent, the classifications themselves group together by who authorized the text. Other times it's hard to distinguish. Humor, if intentional, is usually supplied by the deceased; likewise quotes. Romantic expressions and eulogies are more often offered by the survivors. Poignancies probably come after the fact, whereas advice is probably contemplated well in advance.

Where I tried to make a determination was as to the source of the epitaph itself: who wrote it? Without doing a count to determine properly, I'd estimate that half or better of the epitaphs in this collection were written by other than the deceased or an intimate survivor, that the epitaph was borrowed from an independent source. You'll note the chapter heading "Borrowed Mournings" is further broken down into eleven subcategories depending on from where the lines originated. It seemed of interest to know what the source was, as that would supply information about the deceased, what struck their fancy and/or was popular in their day.

Following "Borrowed Mournings" come two other categories of non-original epitaphs: biblical and what I call "palliatives." I originally termed them "bromides" but decided that was a little too pejorative. A "palliative" is something that doesn't cure one but makes them feel better. What more can one hope for with an epitaph for a lost loved one? Many palliatives are found in collections designed for just that purpose: providing epitaphs. They exist currently on the Web and have undoubtedly been around the funeral business for generations. For the most part, their authorship is unknown or, occasionally, incorrectly attributed.

The range of sources is astounding: rock & roll; pop songs; hymns; country-western ballads; poets of all stripe; religious mystics; slogans; prayers; philosophers; and, of course, the Bible and the Bard.

Most quotes are unattributed, which likely reflects the added cost of lettering or room on the stone. I am sure there are as yet unattributed epitaphs in this collection simply because I was unable to track down their sources. That's what dear readers are for.

Needless-to-say, categorization was subjective. Many epitaphs could fit in multiple categories and sometimes determination had to be made by age of the deceased or the time-period of their death. Enigmas can be amusing; advice can be romantic; the romantic can become poignant. Sometimes, while transcribing the epitaphs for little children, I had to stop and turn away from the computer. I can never read the epitaph, "It will be okay," without thinking, "No, it won't." Sometimes I wonder why I do this. But then I get to the romantic ones and I swoon with the old lovers all over again. I read the epitaphs of old people dying and seeing for one last moment what the world looked like through their eyes when they were young.

With the exception of quoted material, I have left most epitaphs unannotated; and I believe I did the annotating of the quotes because I could, not because it was absolutely necessary. Nonetheless, as I said, I felt that understanding the source would help understand the deceased. What song was the deceased listening to when they were twenty-two?

How the categories got arranged depended on how it was most useful to look at them. My default organization was alphabetical by first lines, but that was frequently overruled. Shakespeare is arranged by the source play from which the quote is taken, and the plays are listed alphabetically. If a play has multiple quotes, they are arranged alphabetically by first lines. Palliatives, on the other hand, are arranged by

4

date of the deceased (or birth, if only that is known). That was because the temporal transition of styles is so significant. Likewise, the style of eulogies shifts dramatically over time, so it was important to arrange them chronologically, as well; whereas the categories of romantic and humorous epitaphs have virtually no non-modern dates, so they, too, are arranged by first lines. The Bible got sorted by order in which the quote appears. Advice, enigmas, "Final Touches," are all sorted by first lines.

Broadly speaking, there are three periods of epitaph styles in Oregon Territory cemeteries: early, interregnum, and modern. "Early" began in the late 1830s and extended through the turn of the century into the nineteen-teens and twenties, a period of god-fearing conformity and the reign of piety. Some of the best eulogies—often written decades later—come from this time. It was definitely a Christian army that rolled over the West.

The interregnum takes over in the thirties and lasts until the 1970s. This is the era of the gray flannel suit and tombstones to match. The floridity of the past was replaced by a taciturn bunch willing to settle for names and dates only. Cost may have been a factor, but as much as anything, cemeteries went out of style. The nation turned its back on death. The World Wars didn't help. Modernity came booming in and by the time the 50s came rolling around, nobody wanted to remember as far back as the 40s. Consequently, epitaphs waned. Lawn cemeteries spread like noxious weeds.

Then there were hippies and LSD and suddenly the world became much more holistic and the past was revived from its premature death. Floridity returned. Humor and sentiment bloomed. The paucity of the interregnum was replaced by something other than the pious gloom of the formative years. All of a sudden, epitaphs were supposed to reflect the person interred, not just how society wanted them to be remembered. Epitaphs were now supposed to come from the heart and not the pastor. The business boomed. Cost was again a factor as new technology permitted more for less. (Although "boomed" is a relative term; the whole industry has had a huge falling off in the past decades, thanks to cremation.) The result has been an epitaph collector's dream.

Too bad there aren't more of us. Which, truthfully, surprises me. There's such a large resource simply sitting out there waiting to be mined and it's going nowhere. How can that be? How did we get stuck with a clutch of epitaphs from an odd assortment of people from New or Old England and a handful of movie stars?

This collection casts a much wider net. The criteria for inclusion

5

didn't include fame; it tracked instead the emotions of everyday people irrespective of their notoriety. In this we are truly blessed by modern technology which permits the economical addition of epitaphs to tombstones and by the change in culture which liberated America from its Calvinist upbringing. The result is a much more nuanced picture of the deceased than that filtered through a religious prism. Religion is still there, but it's been joined by a secular chorus. Thirty years ago this would have been a drastically different collection.

Romance, for example, wouldn't have been included. Indeed, in general, the real emotions of older epitaphs can only be hinted at through the veil of chapbook homilies; whereas modern emotions are writ bold on the stone face. The considerable majority of these epitaphs are modern.

Reading epitaphs is akin to reading poetry. It's not like reading a joke book. Epitaphs call for reflection; after all, they are the last call from the dead, they deserve our respect. Even the funny ones. Reading them in big gulps can be numbing, you lose the time to think of who each person was.

What about truth in advertising? Was Thoreau right? Is truth the first casualty of the epitaph? Well, yes, sort of, more or less, maybe. But... It depends, largely, on what you think truth is and what you think the purpose of an epitaph is. On the one hand, it's the distillation of the deceased, no matter who supplied it. It is the turn by which they will be remembered. Think of it as loose-limbed haiku for the dead. No matter what the epitaph, who authored it, or its history, it tells us something about whoever commissioned it. That truth can never be hidden. Whether or not that's the truth the author intended is another matter. Epitaphs are not unlike highway historical markers which say as much or more about who erected them as they do about the historical events themselves.

Were the pioneers as pious as their tombstones would lead us to believe? I doubt it. I'm sure it was as much the fashion of the day to select the appropriate homily as it was to wear the appropriate black tie and suit to a funeral or to have one's tombstone portrait be a solemn studio sitting. Nowadays, a formal portrait is as rare as a casual one was in the 1900s.

This, then, is a record of a people. It's an intimation of how they felt about death and life, what mattered to them, what strings plucked at their hearts.

A note about the notes. You'll run across many references to *Wikipedia*, the lazy man's information guide. I put those references in quotation marks; but a small caveat: I've edited them somewhat for clarity, ease of reading, relevance, length, and congruence with this text. As entries in *Wikipedia* are constantly open to change, you can assume that my references are from around the publication date of this text. The errors that aren't *Wikipedia's* are mine. *Wikipedia* and other Web sources are italicized; their information is in quotes. Is it cheating to cite *Wikipedia* so much? I'll know if their lawyers contact me. Within categories, I have, for the most part, alphabetized the entries by first lines. An exception is that I've tried to keep multiple quotes by the same author together. The name(s) of the interred follows the epitaph.

Punctuation and spelling. Hmm? Were I to put a "sic" after each dropped comma, the text would have been unreadable. As a rule, I don't comment on commas unless their presence or lack alters the meaning of the epitaph. (My favorite dropped comma is in [or is not in, as the case may be] the epitaph "You don't know boys." See what I mean? How about girls? Do I know girls? What do you say, boys and girls?) I do note dropped or gratuitous apostrophes, though, and egregious spelling errors.

❖

The Oregon Territory is vast and varied. It harbors some of the driest and some of the wettest places in America. It has "mountains and rivers without end." It has broad stretches where no one lives, high deserts that snatch the life from the unwary, volcanic mountain ranges buried in winter snows, gorges that have no bottoms, forests deep and dank, rivers that have no return. It has fanciful cities and abundant farm land. It breasts the Pacific Ocean and suckles the winds that roar in from the sea.

Still, it's of a piece and we recognize the people passing by as we walk the streets of each other's towns. For the most part, we die in the English language and have all listened to the same radio stations. We laughed at the same sit-coms and cheered the same teams. We had the same teachers in the same high schools. We are a people, whether born to the land or drawn here by fate. We inhale the same salt air and the same wind-borne dust.

Whoever we were, some of us have left a message carved into

stone to lie softly through the generations, that others should came and see and know that we were here. That we were alive. That we had souls. That we sang. That though long departed, our voices are still heard.

Listen.

BORROWED MOURNINGS

It's long been a practice of using someone else's words to adorn one's headstone. In the early period (1830-1930) epitaphs were invariably chapbook homilies, now blurring under weathering and hard to decipher. The stilted language oft found on these headstones harks back to an earlier era with a gloss of greater piety. The pressures to use these maudlin phrases must have been great, for between them and the studio portraits, it's hard to find the real person. What one finds on early (our scale) tombstones reflects more of the culture than the individual which is carefully overlaid with a veneer of conventionality.

I call that style of epitaphs "palliatives." I've separated them out from other quoted sources along with the *Bible*. For the most part, their authors are unknown.

"Borrowed Mournings" are epitaphs taken from known sources, attributed or not, which I've divided into eleven categories and arranged by first lines. Their range is astounding, from Captain Tom to Led Zepplin and Buddy Holly. Harry Dixon Loes to Squire Parsons. Writers such as Robert Frost, Edgar Guest, Thomas Wolfe, and William Cullen Bryant. Lord Tennyson, Dylan Thomas, and Robert Burns. Not to mention Shakespeare. Mystics, saints, and stern New England moralists, along with a small smattering of children's authors who deserve a much larger place, if you ask me.

These epitaphs are primarily modern. One presumes they are most often selected by the deceased as emblematic of who they were. Compared to the homilies of the early period, they expose a diverse and contemplative society, one that gives thought to what it leaves behind. We have changed; and from the cemeterian's viewpoint, for the better. At least for the more interesting.

This book could not have been assembled without Google. In pre-Google days, it would have taken years longer tracking down sources. It, perhaps, couldn't have been reasonably done. As it is, whenever I came across a suspiciously well-worded epitaph, I'd throw it into Google and see what showed up. Bingo! I'm sure there were ones I missed, but I certainly caught enough to give a feeling for what a wide net cast among the tombstones will bring in.

POP SONGS

And the wind will
Whisper her name to me.

And the wind will whisper your name to me.

John Denver, "For Baby (For Bobbie)." The song was first released on the album *Rocky Mountain High*.

Sierra Skye Carlson (1986-1986)
Hillcrest-Hillcrest East Cemetery

Are you ready to go, do you want to go on the Wonder
Bus...
The song is ended but the Melody lingers on.

Beda Loehner, lyrics, in 1927 with music by Irving Berlin, "The Song is Ended (but the Melody Lingers On)." The first line of the epitaph is lifted from elsewhere, but I haven't been able to track it down. *Wikipedia*: "Irving Berlin (1888-1989) was a Russian-born American composer and lyricist widely considered one of the greatest songwriters in American history. He published his first song, 'Marie from Sunny Italy,' in 1907 and had his first major international hit, 'Alexander's Ragtime Band,' in 1911."

Richard Vazquez (1967-2004)
Saint Mary's Cemetery (Corvallis)

Because you come to me with naught save love
And hold my hand and lift mine eyes above,
A wider world of hope and joy I see,
Because you come to me.

Because you speak to me in accents sweet
I find roses walking "round my feet,
And I am led through tears of joy to thee
Because you speak to me.

Because God made thee mine I'll cherish thee
Through light and darkness, through all time to be,
And pray his love may make our love divine,
Because God made thee mine.

Edward Teschemacher; lyrics; music by Guy d'Hardelot (1902). "Because," recorded by Perry Como in 1947. *YouTube*: "Released on the 1959 album *Harry Secombe Sings the Favourite Songs of Richard Tauber*. Enrico Caruso had a hit with his recording of the song during the early part of the 1900s."

Dean (1928-2000) & Mary (b. 1928) Gipson
Mountain View Memorial

Believe it or not, I'm walking on air
I never thought I could feel so free

Stephen Geyer, lyrics, and music by Mike Post. "Believe It or Not," theme song for *Greatest American Hero* TV show. *Wikipedia*: "*The Greatest American Hero* was an American comedy-drama television series that aired for three seasons from 1981 to 1983 on ABC."

Benjamin Hauptman (1978-2009)
Pacific Sunset Cemetery

Between now and then
Till I see you again,
I'll be loving you

12

Love, Me
Christian, Samantha, Rylie

And between now and then, till I see you again,
I'll be loving you. Love, me.

Collin Raye, "Love, Me." *Wikipedia*: "Floyd Elliott Wray (b. 1960 in De Queen, Arkansas) is an American country music singer, known professionally as Collin Raye. He made his debut on the American country music scene in 1991 with the release of his album *All I Can Be*, which produced his first Number One hit in 'Love, Me.'"

Benoit
Canyon Hill Cemetery

Earth, below me drifting floating
floating weightless going home

Earth below us, drifting falling
Floating weightless, calling calling home

Peter Schilling, "Major Tom (Coming Home)." Major Tom, a fictional astronaut, was created by David Bowie and used in a number of his songs. The character was taken up and expanded on by other artists, including Peter Schilling.

Jack Dempsey (1929-1997)
Yamhill-Carlton Cemetery

Either let me fly or give me death
Let my soul rest or take my breath

Either let me fly, or give me death
Let my soul rest, take my breath

"Let Me Fly," performed by DMX. *Wikipedia*: "Earl Simmons (b. 1970), better known by his stage name, DMX (also known as Dog Man X and Dark Man X), is a multi-platinum American rapper and actor. The song is from *It's Dark and Hell Is Hot*, produced by Dame Grease and Young Lord and written by Earl Simmons, Damon J. Blackman, and Manuel Alejandro. *It's Dark and Hell Is Hot* is the debut album of DMX, released in 1998."

Shane Cooke (1972-1999)
Berge Cemetery

He will raise you up on eagle's wings,
Bear you on the breath of dawn,
Make you to shine like the sun,
And hold you in the palm of His Hand

Josh Groban (b. 1981), "On Eagle's Wings." *Wikipedia*: "Joshua Winslow 'Josh' Groban

13

is an American singer, songwriter, musician, actor, and record producer."

Bradley Anderson (1965-1990)
Wind River Memorial

Home on the range

Brewster M. Higley, lyrics with music by Daniel E. Kelley. *Wikipedia*: "'Home on the Range' is the state song of Kansas. Dr. Brewster M. Higley (1823–1911) originally wrote the words in a poem called 'My Western Home' in the early 1870s in Smith County, Kansas. The poem was first published in a December 1873 issue of the *Smith County Pioneer* under the title 'Oh, Give Me a Home Where the Buffalo Roam.' The music was written by a friend of Higley's, Daniel E. Kelley. Higley's original words are similar to those of the song today but not identical. The song was adopted by settlers, cowboys, and others and spread across the USA in various forms. During the early 20th century, it was arranged by Texas composer David W. Guion (1892–1981) who is often credited as the composer. It was officially adopted as the state song of Kansas on June 30, 1947, and is commonly regarded as the unofficial anthem of the American West."

Stuart Rees (1903-1982)
Coles Valley Cemetery

It was no accident, me finding you
Someone had a hand in it, long before we ever knew

Tracy Byrd, "The Keeper of the Stars." *Wikipedia*: "'The Keeper of the Stars' was recorded by American country music artist Tracy Byrd. Released in early 1995 as the last single from his 1994 album, *No Ordinary Man*, it went on to reach #2 on the Billboard 'Hot Country Singles & Tracks' charts. A year after its release, it was named Song of the Year by the Country Music Association."

Robert (1949-2002) & Susan Sturm (b. 1949)
Joseph Cemetery

Love, good night must thou go when
the day and the night need the [sic] so
All is well, hasten all to their rest

Horace Lorenzo Trim, "Taps," 7th verse. *Wikipedia*: "The term originates from the Dutch term *taptoe*, meaning 'close the (beer) taps (and send the troops back to camp).' The tune is a variation of an earlier bugle call known as the 'Scott Tattoo' which was used in the U.S. from 1835 until 1860 and was arranged in its present form by the Union Army Brigadier General Daniel Butterfield an American Civil War general and Medal of Honor recipient who commanded the 3rd Brigade of the 1st Division in the V Army Corps of the Army of the Potomac while at Harrison's Landing, Virginia, in July, 1862 to replace a previous French bugle call used to signal 'lights out.' Butterfield's bugler, Oliver W. Norton, of Erie, Pennsylvania, was the first to sound the new call. Within months, 'Taps' was used by both Union and Confederate forces. It was officially recognized by the United States Army in 1874."

Wm. (1894-1926) & Edna Goheen (1898-1987)
Firhill Cemetery

Nothing compares to you

Prince, "Nothing Compares 2 U." *Wikipedia*: "Sinéad Marie Bernadette O'Connor (b. 1966) is an Irish singer-songwriter who rose to fame in the late 1980s with her debut album *The Lion and the Cobra*. O'Connor achieved worldwide success in 1990 with a cover of 'Nothing Compares 2 U' which was written by Prince for his side-project *The Family*."

Kevin Fawcett (1960-1990)
Frank Abel Cemetery

One more day
One more time
One more
sunset maby [sic]
I'd be satisfied, but then
again I know
what it would do, leave
me wishing still for
one more day with
you

One more day, One more time
One more sunset maybe I'd be satisfied
But then again; I know what it would do
Leave me wishing still, for one more day with you

Lonestar, "One More Day" (2001). *Wikipedia*: "Lonestar is an American country music group which began in 1992 as a band named Texassee."

Anon
Rock Point/Gold Hill IOOF Cemetery

Put my picture in your pocket
So I'll be close to you.
No more will I be lonesome
And no more will I be blue.
And when we have to part dear
There will be no sad ado [sic].
For I'll be in your pocket
And I'll go along with you.

Put me in your pocket so I'll be close to you
No more will I be lonesome and no more will I be blue

And when we have to part, dear, there'll be no sad adieu
For I'll be in your pocket and I'll go along with you

Hank Locklin, "Put me in Your Pocket" first appears on the album *The Girls Get Prettier* (1966). *Wikipedia*: "Lawrence Hankins Locklin (1918-2009), better known as Hank Locklin, was an American country music singer-songwriter. A member of the Grand Ole Opry for nearly 50 years, Locklin had a long recording career with RCA Victor and scored big with the hits, 'Please Help Me, I'm Falling,' 'Send Me the Pillow That You Dream On,' and 'Geisha Girl', from 1957-60. His singles charted from 1949-71."

> Lawrence (b. 1931) & Ramona Bailey (b. 1936)
> Fir Grove Cemetery

She is handsome, she is pretty
She is the belle of Belfast city

Traditional Irish song, also known as "I'll Tell Me Ma" or "Tell My Ma" or some such variation.

> Doreen Allen (1923-1997)
> Mother Joseph Catholic Cemetery

She sang in the sunshine

Wikipedia: "Gale Zoë Garnett (b. 1942) is a New Zealand-born, Canadian singer best known in the United States for her 1964 Grammy-winning folk hit 'We'll Sing in the Sunshine.'"

> Nina Kennedy (1921-1989)
> Mosier Cemetery

Sweet William, Know our love will not fade away

I'm a gonna tell you how it's going to be
You're gonna give your love to me
I wanna love you night and day
You know my love will not fade away
You know my love will not fade away

"Not Fade Away," 1957; Buddy Holly and Norman Petty, "The Chirping Crickets."

> William Weintraub (1963-1995)
> Havurah Shalom Cemetery

The Queen of Light
Took her bow
And then she turned to gold
The Prince of Peace
Embraced the Queen

16

And warmed the night for all

The Queen of Light took her bow and then she turned to go
The Prince of Peace embraced the gloom and walked the night alone

Led Zeppelin, "The Battle for Evermore." *Wikipedia*: "Led Zeppelin was an English rock band, active in the late 1960s and throughout the 1970s, formed as the New Yardbirds in 1968. 'The Battle of Evermore' by Robert Plant and Jimmy Page is featured on their untitled fourth album (a.k.a. *Led Zeppelin IV*) released in 1971."

Jill Lynch (1965-1982)
Colton Lutheran Cemetery

The sweetest thing
We ever knew
Was loving you.

The sweetest thing
I've ever known
Is lovin' you

Juice Newton, "The Sweetest Thing" (1983). *Wikipedia*: "Judy Kay 'Juice' Newton (b. 1952, Lakehurst, NJ) is an American pop and country singer, songwriter, and guitarist. To date, Newton has received five Grammy Award nominations in the Pop and Country Best Female Vocalist categories (winning once in 1983)."

Ronald Curtis 1965-1982)
Bunker Hill Cemetery

'Til the Twelfth of Never

Jerry Livingston and Paul Francis Webster. "The Twelfth of Never" was recorded by Johnny Mathis in 1957.

Lavaun (1933-1996) & Emagene Koch (b. 1937)
Crescent Grove Cemetery

To know him is
To love him

Phil Spector. *Wikipedia*: "'To Know Him Is to Love Him' was written by Phil Spector, inspired by words on his father's tombstone, 'To Know Me Is To Love Me.' First recorded by his first vocal group, the only one of which he was a member, the Teddy Bears. Their recording went to number one on the *Billboard* Hot 100 singles chart in 1958. The Beatles recorded it as 'To Know Her Is to Love Her,' although their version wasn't officially released until their 1994 *Live at the BBC* compilation album. Marc Bolan and Gloria Jones, Gary Glitter, Peter and Gordon, and Bobby Vinton made versions called 'To Know You Is to Love You.' In 1987 the song was resurrected by Dolly Parton, Linda Ronstadt and Emmylou Harris, whose *Trio* recording topped the U.S. country singles charts."

Grant Large (1957-1997)
Pacific Sunset Cemetery

We built a sweet little nest, somewhere out in the west,
and let the rest of the world go by

Out there beneath a kindly sky
We'll build a sweet little nest somewhere in the west
And let the rest of the world go by.

J. Keirn Brennan, lyrics and music by Ernest R. Ball. *GrowingBolder.com*: "'Let the Rest of the World Go By' debuted in 1919. It was recorded by Dick Haymes in 1944 and used in the soundtrack for the 1985 movie *Out of Africa*."

Rosie (1933-1999) & Don (b. 1930) Bray
Spring Valley Presbyterian Cemetery

You are the promised kiss of springtime that makes the
lonely winter seem long
You are the breathless hush of evening that trembles on the
brink of a lovely song
You are the angel glow that lights a star, the dearest
things I know are what you are

Oscar Hammerstein II, lyrics, and music by Jerome Kern. *Wikipedia*: "Oscar Greeley Clendenning Hammerstein II (1895–1960) was an American librettist, theatrical producer, and (usually uncredited) theatre director of musicals for almost forty years. 'All the Things You Are' was composed for the musical *Very Warm for May* (1939)."

Patrick Martin (b. 1949) & Robert Rusk (1959-2002)
Ocean View Cemetery

You're in my heart, you're in my soul. You'll be my breath,
should I grow old.
You are my lover, you're my best friend, you're in my soul.

Rod Stewart. *Wikipedia*: "'You're in My Heart (The Final Acclaim)' was written and recorded by Rod Stewart for his 1977 album *Foot Loose & Fancy Free*."

Rusty Kimball (1951-1997)
Mountain View Memorial Gardens

CHRISTIAN SONGS

And grace will lead me home

Through many dangers, toils and snares, I have already come
Twas grace that brought me safe thus far and grace will lead me home.

John Newton penned this familiar third verse to "Amazing Grace." *Wikipedia*: "John Henry Newton (1725–1807) was a British sailor and Anglican clergyman. Starting his career at sea at a young age, he became involved with the slave trade for a few years, and was himself enslaved for a period. After experiencing a religious conversion, he became a minister, hymn-writer, and later a prominent supporter of the abolition of slavery. He was the author of many hymns, including 'Amazing Grace' and 'Glorious Things of Thee are Spoken.'"

Mary Schreindle (1934-1994)
Mountain Home Cemetery

Blessed be the tie that binds

John Fawcett (1740-1817). Title of a song written in 1772 by the English evangelist and preacher.

George (1892-1982) & Laura (1892-1993) Appel
Damascus Cemetery

Down by the sea, the crystal sea, where all of the redeemed shall be. Where you and I, Beloved, shall go. Our crimson robes washed white as snow in Christ's dear blood—what hymns of praise through countless ages we shall raise! There all our loved ones we shall see—think what a meeting that will be down by the sea!

"Down by the Sea" from *Songs by the Sea* by Rebecca Springer, 1889.

Joan (1947-1986) & Wayne (b. 1948)
Lone Oak Cemetery

*Far away in the depths of my Spirit to-night,
Rolls a melody sweeter than psalm;
In celestial like strains it unceasingly falls
O'er my soul like an infinite calm.*

Far away in the depths of my spirit tonight
Rolls a melody sweeter than psalm;
In celestial strains it unceasingly falls
O'er my soul like an infinite calm.

Warren D. Cornell (1858-1901), "Wonderful Peace" (1889). In 1880 he was identified in the census as "Minister of the Gospel."

Anon

19

God of the earth, the sky, the sea
Maker of all above, below
Creation lives and moves in thee. Thy present
life through all doth flow

God of the earth, the sky, the sea!
Maker of all above, below!
Creation lives and moves in Thee,
Thy present life in all doth flow.

Samuel Longfellow, *Hymns of the Spirit* (1864). Samuel was a brother of Henry Wadsworth Longfellow.

Lee (1914-1997) & Dana Whipple (1915-2005)
Applegate Pioneer Cemetery

His eye is on the sparrow
And I know He watches me

Civilla D. Martin, "His Eye Is on the Sparrow." *Wikipedia*: "'His Eye Is on the Sparrow' is a Gospel hymn. Although today it is a staple of African-American worship services, the song was originally written in 1905 by two white songwriters, lyricist Civilla D. Martin and composer Charles H. Gabriel. The song is most associated with actress-singer Ethel Waters who used the title for her autobiography."

Dian Kern (1940-2005)
Yachats Memorial Park

In the sweet bye and bye

Samuel F. Bennett (1836-1898), "In the Sweet Bye and Bye" (1868); hymn by Bennett and J. P. Webster.

Mildred Roberts (1932-1995)
Yankton Community Fellowship Cemetery

It is well with my soul

Horatio Gates Spafford (1828-1888), "It Is Well With My Soul." Horatio Gates Spafford was a prominent American lawyer, best known for penning the Christian hymn "It Is Well With My Soul," following a family tragedy in which four of his daughters died.

Janice Ross (1952-1992)
Hills Cemetery

I've been homesick for a city,
To which I'd never been before;

No sad goodbyes here will be spoken,
For time doesn't matter anymore.

Beulah Land, I've been longing for you,
And now on thee I'll stand;
Here my home shall be eternal,
Beulah Land, sweet Beulah Land.

I'm kind of homesick for a country
To which I've never been before.
No sad goodbyes will there be spoken
for time won't matter anymore.

(Chorus)

Beulah Land, I'm longing for you
and some day on thee I'll stand.
There my home shall be eternal.
Beulah Land -- Sweet Beulah Land.

Squire Parsons. Parsons recorded the Southern gospel song "Sweet Beulah Land" (1973) in 1979.

Lavona (1938-2006) & Donald Schroder (b. 1939)
Zion Memorial Cemetery

Resting high upon the mountain,
Their work on earth is done.

Go rest high on that mountain
Son, your work on earth is done
Go to heaven a shoutin'
Love for the Father and the Son

Vince Gill, "Go Rest High on that Mountain." *Taste of Country*: "Initially written by Vince Gill in response to the passing of country legend Keith Whitley in 1989, the song earned Gill a pair of Grammy Awards in 1996, including Best Country Song, and also helped the prolific songwriter win the CMA Song of the Year trophy the same year."

Gregory Clements (1961-1996)
Fern Hill Cemetery

Seize the day
Seize whatever you can
'Cause life slips away just like hourglass sand
Seize the day
Pray for grace from God's hand
Then nothing will stand in your way

21

Seize the day

Carolyn Arends (b. 1968), "Seize the Day," released 2000. *Wikipedia*: "Carolyn Arends is a contemporary Christian musician, songwriter, and author based in Surrey, British Columbia, Canada."

Dustin Klaus 1981-1998)
Evergreen Memorial

The consecrated cross he did bear;
Till death did set him free,
And then went home his crown to wear
With everlasting glee.

The consecrated cross I'll bear
till death shall set me free;
and then go home my crown to wear,
for there's a crown for me.

George N. Allen, "Must Jesus Bear the Cross Alone?" Thomas Shepherd wrote the first verse (1693). Verse two was written anonymously at an unknown date. Verse three, the verse in question, was penned by Allen in 1844. The final two verses were added by Henry W. Beecher in 1855.

Anon
St Paul's Catholic Cemetery

This little light of mine, I'm going to let it shine,
let it shine, let it shine...

Harry Dixon Loes. *Hymnary.org*: "Harry Dixon Loes (1895-1965). Born Harold Loes, the American gospel song writer took the middle name 'Dixon' in honour of A. C. Dixon, the pastor of Moody Church at the time. Loes studied at Moody Bible Institute; and after extensive training in music, he served a number of churches with a ministry of music. From 1939 until his retirement, he was a member of the music faculty of Moody Bible Institute. He wrote the lyrics for 1,500 gospel songs and composed 3,000 tunes."

Wikipedia reports, "The song has since entered the folk tradition, first being collected by John Lomax in 1939. Often thought of as a Negro spiritual, it does not, however, appear in any collection of jubilee or plantation songs from the nineteenth century."

Marilyn Strycker (1940-2006)
Bandon Lodge #133 IOOF Cemetery

Til my trophies
At last I
Lay down

George Bennard (1873-1958). "The Old Rugged Cross" is a popular Christian song written in 1912 by the evangelist cum song-leader.

Safotu
Siskiyou Memorial Park

We can cry with hope
We can say goodbye with hope
'Cause we know our goodbye
Is not the end.
And we can grieve with hope
'Cause we believe with hope
There's a place by God's grace
Where we'll see your face again.

Stephen Curtis Chapman (b. 1962), "With Hope." Christian rock artist (musical variety). *Wikipedia*: "*Speechless* is the ninth studio album from Chapman. It was released in 1999 by Sparrow Records and is considered, by many, one of Chapman's greater works. It's recognized as being one of the best Christian albums of all time."

Cheung Lung (1961-2001)
River View Cemetery

When we all get to heaven what a
day of rejoicing that will be

Eliza Hewitt, lyrics with music by Emily Wilson, "When We All Get to Heaven" (1898).

Letha Buehler (b. 1929)
Walton Cemetery

Whenever I touch a velvet rose
Or walk by a lilac tree,
I'll remember you came into this beautiful world
And shared these creations with me

Whenever I touch a velvet rose
Or walk by our lilac tree,
I'm glad that I live in this beautiful world
Heav'nly Father created for me.

Clara W. McMaster (1904–1997), "My Heavenly Father Loves Me." From *Children's Songbook of The Church of Jesus Christ of Latter-day Saints* (1989).

Charolette Mae Roses (1990-1995)
Adams Cemetery

AMERICAN AUTHORS

A river runs through it

Title of Norman MacLean's 1976 book. *Furman.edu*: "The phrase a river runs through it is biblical in origin. It is part of the description of Eden in the *Book of Genesis*." I don't know if that's true or not, but MacLean's book remains one of the finest books in the American language. The movie was nice, but the pictures in the book were better.

> Hall
> Peaceful Hill Cemetery

> *Across the years I*
> *will walk with*
> *you in deep*
> *green forest; on*
> *shores of sand*
> *and when our*
> *time on earth is*
> *through, in heaven,*
> *too, you will have*
> *my hand.*

"The Promise," Robert Sexton. On his Website, Mr. Sexton calls himself "an American romantic." He combines his poetry with self-drawn illustrations which he offers for sale on his site. In his words, "This piece is called 'The Promise.' After writing the poem, I worked with a quill pen to create a gift in honor of my youngest brother and his wife."

> Thomas (1934-2000) & Gayle Spear (b. 1936)
> Ocean View Cemetery

> *"Away"*

> *I can not say & I will not*
> *Say that he is dead —*
> *He is just away.*

> *With a cheery smile & a wave of*
> *The hand,*
> *He has wandered into an unknown*
> *Land.*
> *James Whitcomb Riley*

I cannot say, and I will not say
That he is dead--. He is just away!

With a cheery smile, and a wave of the hand
He has wandered into an unknown land,

And left us dreaming how very fair
It needs must be, since he lingers there.

James Whitcomb Riley (1849-1916). *Wikipedia*: "An American writer, poet, and best-selling author, during his lifetime he was known as the Hoosier Poet and Children's Poet for his dialect works and his children's poetry respectively. His poems tended to be humorous or sentimental, and of the approximately one thousand poems that Riley authored, the majority are in dialect. His famous works include 'Little Orphant Annie' and 'The Raggedy Man.'"
    I've seen the last two stanzas as an epitaph, as well.

Russell Bender
Mount Jefferson Memorial Park

Here was a man to hold against the world,
A man to match the mountains and the sea

Edwin Markam, "Lincoln, Man of the People." *Commandposts.com*: "This poem was chosen out of two-hundred-fifty Lincoln poems, by the committee headed by Chief Justice Taft, to be read at the dedication of the Lincoln Memorial in Washington, D.C., in 1922. One-hundred-thousand people were present and two-million more were listening in on the radio. President Warren Harding delivered the address, and Edwin Markham read his poem."
    Wikipedia: "Charles Edwin Anson Markham (1852-1940) was an American poet. From 1923 to 1931 he was Poet Laureate of Oregon."

Richard Baum (1923-1980)
Hillcrest-Hillcrest East Cemetery

I am standing upon the seashore.
A ship, at my side spreads her white sails
to the moving breeze and starts for the blue ocean.
She is an object of beauty and strength.
I stand and watch her until, at length, she hangs like
a speck of white cloud just where the sea and sky
come to mingle with each other.
Then, someone at my side says, "There, she is gone!"
Gone where?
Gone from my sight. That is all.
She is just as large in mast and hull and spar
as she was when she left my side
and she is just as able to bear her load
of living freight to her destined port.
Her diminished size is in me, not in her.

25

And just at the moment when someone at my side says:
"There, she is gone!"
There are other eyes watching her coming,
and other voices ready to take up the glad shout:
"Here she comes!"
And that is dying.

Henry Van Dyke, "I Am Standing upon the Seashore." The poem is pretty close to how Van Dyke wrote it. Close enough. *Wikipedia*: "Henry Jackson van Dyke (1852-1933) was an American author, educator, and clergyman. By appointment of President Wilson, he became Minister to the Netherlands and Luxembourg in 1913."

Another site referred to him as an "American short-story writer, poet and essayist."

Anon
Haines Cemetery

I catch the pattern of your
silence before you speak
I do not need to hear a word,
In your silence: every tone
I seek is heard

Langston Hughes, "Silence" (1941). *Wikipedia*: "James Mercer Langston Hughes (1902-1967) was an American poet, social activist, novelist, playwright, and columnist. He was one of the earliest innovators of the then-new literary art form, jazz poetry. Hughes is best known for his work during the Harlem Renaissance. He famously wrote about the period that 'the negro was in vogue' which was later paraphrased as 'when Harlem was in vogue.'"

Bernard (1926-1993) & Elaine (1931-2004) Pirotsky
Ahavai Shalom Cemetery

I have promises to keep
And miles to go before I sleep

"I have promises to keep,
And miles to go before I sleep.

Robert Frost. *Wikipedia*: "Robert Lee Frost (1874-1963) was an American poet highly regarded for his realistic depictions of rural life and his command of American colloquial speech. One of the most popular and critically respected American poets of his generation, Frost was honored frequently during his lifetime, receiving four Pulitzer Prizes for Poetry. 'Stopping by Woods on a Snowy Evening' was written in 1922 and published in 1923 in Frost's *New Hampshire* volume."

David Quiring Jr. (1905-1969)
Evergreen-Washelli Cemetery

Two roads diverged in a wood, and
I took the one less traveled by,
And that made all the difference.
        Robert Frost

"The Road Not Taken," from the Robert Frost collection, *Mountain Interval* (1920).

James (1928-2000) & Dorothy (b. 1930) Ashbaugh
River View Cemetery

...I sleep in my earth
    like a tired fox,
And my buffalo have
    found me.
        S. V. Benet

Go play with the towns you have built of blocks,
The towns where you would have bound me!
I sleep in my earth like a tired fox,
And my buffalo have found me.

Stephen Vincent Benét. Last two lines of "The Ballad of William Sycamore," (1922). *Wikipedia*: "Stephen Vincent Benét (1898-1943) was an American author, poet, short story writer, and novelist. Benét is best known for his book-length narrative poem of the American Civil War, *John Brown's Body* (1928), for which he won a Pulitzer Prize in 1929, and for two short stories, 'The Devil and Daniel Webster' (1936) and 'By the Waters of Babylon' (1937)."

William Gray II (1925-1976)
Fort Klamath Cemetery

I thought, I should not see these dunes again
Or feel the sting of this wind bitten land,
Where the grasses all blow one way
Bent, like my thoughts, by an unseen hand.

I thought I should not walk these dunes again,
Nor feel the sting of this wind-bitten sand,
Where the coarse grasses always blow one way,
Bent, as my thoughts are, by an unseen hand.

"Sand Drift" Sara Teasdale (1884-1933) from *Dark of the Moon* (1940). *Wikipedia*: "Sara Teasdale was an American lyrical poet. She was born Sara Trevor Teasdale in St. Louis, Missouri, and after her marriage in 1914 she went by the name Sara Teasdale Filsinger."

Joseph DeLorme Jr. (1941-1973)
Chief Schonchin Cemetery

I'll lend you for a little time a child of mine

Edgar Guest, "I'll Lend You a Child." *Wikipedia*: "Edgar Albert Guest (1881-1959), aka Eddie Guest, was a prolific English-born American poet who was popular in the first half of the 20th century and became known as the People's Poet."

Kathleen (1964-1970) & Eileen Purdy (1966-1970)
Visitation Cemetery

Miss me
But let me go

"Miss Me—But Let Me Go!" Poem by Edgar Guest.

James Cameron Jr. (1921-2002)
Willamette National Cemetery

Into my heart's treasury I slipped a coin
that time cannot take nor thief purloin
Oh, better than the minting of a gold-crowned king
is the safe kept memory of a lovely thing

Sara Teasdale, "The Coin" (1920). *Wikipdeia*: "Sara Teasdale (1884-1933) was an American lyrical poet. She was born Sara Trevor Teasdale in St. Louis, Missouri, and after her marriage in 1914 she went by the name Sara Teasdale Filsinger.

"A common urban legend surrounds Teasdale's suicide. The legend claims that her poem 'I Shall Not Care' (which features themes of abandonment, bitterness, and contemplation of death) was penned as a suicide note to a former lover. However, the poem was actually first published in her 1915 collection *Rivers to the Sea*, a full eighteen years before her suicide."

Nedra Howell (1939-1991)
Mountain View - Corbett

It is my prayer, it is my longing, that we may pass from this life together - a longing which shall never perish from the earth, but shall have a place in the heart of every wife that loves, until the end of time; and it shall be called by my name.

But if one of us must go first, it is my prayer that it shall be I; for he is strong, I am weak, I am not so necessary to him as he is to me - life without him would not be life; how could I endure it? This prayer is also immortal, and will not cease from being offered up while my race continues. I am the first wife; and in the last wife I shall be repeated.

Wheresoever she was, there was Eden.

Mark Twain, *Eve's Diary* (1906). Exactly what the title is of the work from which this was extracted is somewhat confusing; nonetheless, Project Gutenburg provides the entire *Eve's Diary* from which the epitaph is, apparently, taken. It this case, it is Adam speaking at Eve's grave. She was, it was said, the apple of his eye.

Wikipdeia: "The book version of the story was published with fifty-five illustrations by Lester Ralph, [one] on each left hand page. The illustrations depicted Eve and Adam in their natural settings. The depiction of an unclothed woman was considered pornographic when the book was first released in the United States and created a controversy around the book. One library in Charlton, Massachusetts, banned the book for the depictions of Eve in 'summer costume.'" Twain's defense was that he only wrote the book, he didn't draw the pictures. Still and all, he liked them.

Denise (1958-1992) & Gregory (1952-1997) Nowa
Fir Grove Cemetery

Joy, Shipmate, Joy!
(Pleas'd to my soul at death I cry.)
Our life is closed, our life begins,
The long, long anchorage we leave,
The ship is clear at last, she leaps!
She swiftly courses from the shore.
Joy, shipmate, joy.
   Walt Whitman

Walt Whitman (1819–1892), "Joy, Shipmate, Joy!" *Leaves of Grass*, (1900). *Wikipedia*: "Walter 'Walt' Whitman (1819-1892) was an American poet, essayist and journalist. A humanist, he was a part of the transition between transcendentalism and realism, incorporating both views in his works. Whitman is among the most influential poets in the American canon, often called the father of free verse. His work was very controversial in its time, particularly his poetry collection, *Leaves of Grass*, which was described as obscene for its overt sexuality."

Michael O'Brien (1944-2002)
Saint Mary's Cemetery (Corvallis)

Lives of great men all remind us
   We can make our lives sublime,
And, departing, leave behind us
   Footprints on the sands of time;

Footprints, that perhaps another,
   Sailing o'er life's solemn main,
A forlorn and shipwrecked brother,
   Seeing, shall take heart again.

29

Henry Wadsworth Longfellow

Henry Wadsworth Longfellow. Seventh and eighth stanzas of "A Psalm of Life" (1839). *Wikipedia*: "Henry Wadsworth Longfellow (1807-1882) was an American poet and educator whose works include 'Paul Revere's Ride,' *The Song of Hiawatha*, and *Evangeline*. He was also the first American to translate Dante Alighieri's *The Divine Comedy* and was one of the five Fireside Poets. Longfellow wrote predominantly lyric poems, known for their musicality and often presenting stories of mythology and legend. He became the most popular American poet of his day and also had success overseas."

Henry's brother, Samuel, also provided an epitaph for this volume.

Melvin (1922-1981) & Cleo (b. 1926) Circle
Wisner Cemetery

"Shall I have nought that is fair?" saith he;
"Have nought but the bearded grain?
Though the breath of these flowers is sweet to me,
I will give them all back again."

Henry Wadsworth Longfellow, second verse, "The Reaper and The Flowers" (1838).

Fannie Hamshaw (1868-1894)
Lone Fir Cemetery

My candle burns
at both ends.
It shall not
last the night,
but oh my foes
and friends,
it gives
a lovely light.

My candle burns at both ends;
It will not last the night;
But ah, my foes, and oh, my friends—
It gives a lovely light.

Edna St. Vincent Millay, "First Fig" (1920). *Wikipedia*: "Edna St. Vincent Millay (1892-1950) was an American lyrical poet, playwright and feminist. She received the Pulitzer Prize for Poetry in 1923, the third woman to win the award for poetry, and was also known for her activism and her many love affairs. She used the pseudonym Nancy Boyd for her prose work."

James Mahin (1935-1995)
Mountain View Cemetery

The presence of your absence is everywhere

A. Paul Jewell (1947-1997)
Monument Cemetery

The presence of Dustin's absence is everywhere.

The line, given in varying forms, is attributed to Edna St. Vincent Millay, though I wasn't able to track down the actual source or a definitive quote.

Dustin Klaus (1981-1998)
Evergreen Memorial Cemetery

My pony will soon down his oats
The rising sun will shine
Let's just say this time of day
Should be called "cowboy time"

Last stanza of the poem "Cowboy Time" by Hugh Peltz. Hugh is a Wyoming rancher and cowboy poet.

Tyrel Chandler (1997-2004)
Unknown cemetery in Montana or Idaho

Oh! I have slipped the surly bonds of earth
And danced the skies on laughter-silvered wings;
Sunward I've climbed, and joined the tumbling mirth
Of sun-split clouds - and done a hundred things
You have not dreamed of - wheeled and soared and swung
High in the sunlit silence. Hov'ring there
I've chased the shouting wind along, and flung

My eager craft through footless halls of air.
Up, up the long delirious, burning blue,
I've topped the windswept heights with easy grace
Where never lark, or even eagle flew -
And, while with silent lifting mind I've trod
The high untrespassed sanctity of space,
Put out my hand and touched the face of God.

Gillespie Magee, "High Flight." This poem is not uncommon on pilots' stones. *Wikipedia*: "John Gillespie Magee, Jr. (1922-1941) was an American aviator and poet who died as a result of a mid-air collision over Lincolnshire during World War II. He was serving in the Royal Canadian Air Force which he joined before the United States officially entered the war. He is most famous for this poem. Today it serves as the official poem of the Royal Canadian Air Force and Royal Air Force. It must be recited from memory by fourth class cadets (freshmen) at the United States Air Force Academy (USAFA) where it is also on display in the Cadet Field House."

John Marcum (1980-2001)
Haines Cemetery

Stone-cutters
 fighting time with marble,
 you foredefeated
Challengers of Oblivion
Eat cynical earnings,
  knowing rock splits,
  records fall down,
The square-limbed
  Roman letters
Scale in the thaws,
  wear in the rain.
  The poet as well
Builds his monument mockingly:
For man will be blotted out,
  the blithe earth die,
  the brave sun
Die blind
  and blacken to the heart:
Yet stones have stood
  for a thousand years,
  and pained thoughts found
The honey of peace in old poems.
  R.[obinson] J.[effers]

Robinson Jeffers, "To The Stone-Cutters" in *Tamar and Other Poems* (1924). *Wikipedia*: "John Robinson Jeffers (1887-1962) was an American poet known for his work about the central California coast. Most of Jeffers' poetry was written in classic narrative and epic form, but today he is also known for his short verse and is considered an icon of the environmental movement."

Sara Holzman (1922-2009)
Lone Fir Cemetery (Portland)

The Bridge Builder

An old man going a lone highway,
Came at the evening, cold and gray,
To a chasm vast and deep and wide
Through which was flowing a sullen tide;

32

The old man crossed in the twilight dim,
The sullen stream held no fears for him;
But he turned when safe on the other side
And built a bridge to span the tide.

Old man, said a pilgrim near,
You are wasting strength with building here,
Your journey will end with the ending day;
You will never again pass this way.
You have crossed the chasm deep and wide,
Why build you this bridge at eventide?

The builder lifted his old gray head,
Good friend, in the path I have come, he said,
There followeth after me today
A youth whose feet must pass this way.
This chasm that has been naught to me,
To that fair-haired youth may a pitfall be;
He too must cross in the twilight dim.
Good friend, I am building the bridge for him.

The Bridge Builder

An old man going a lone highway,
Came, at the evening cold and gray,
To a chasm vast and deep and wide.
Through which was flowing a sullen tide
The old man crossed in the twilight dim,
The sullen stream had no fear for him;
But he turned when safe on the other side
And built a bridge to span the tide.

"Old man," said a fellow pilgrim near,
"You are wasting your strength with building here;
Your journey will end with the ending day,
You never again will pass this way;
You've crossed the chasm, deep and wide,
Why build this bridge at evening tide?"

The builder lifted his old gray head;
"Good friend, in the path I have come," he said,
"There followed after me to-day
A youth whose feet must pass this way.
This chasm that has been as naught to me
To that fair-haired youth may a pitfall be;
He, too, must cross in the twilight dim;
Good friend, I am building this bridge for him!"

Will Alan Dromgoole, "The Bridge Builder," from *Father: An Anthology of Verse* (1931). *Wikipedia*: "Will Allen Dromgoole (1860-1934) was an author and poet born in Murfreesboro, Tennessee. She wrote over 7,500 poems, 5,000 essays, and published thirteen books. She was renowned beyond the South; her poem, "The Bridge Builder," was often reprinted. It remains quite popular.

"Dromgoole wrote a series of articles on the Southeastern ethnic group known as the Melungeons, published in the *Nashville Daily American* (1890) and the *Boston Arena* (1891). This historically mixed-race group was then living mostly in southeastern Tennessee and southwestern Kentucky. Her derogatory comments about them, while based more on hearsay than fact, expressed the biases about mountain people typical of her society and the period in which she was writing. Since the early 20th century, Melungeons have increasingly intermarried with European Americans and integrated into mainstream white society."

Ben Gerwick (1883-1977)
Logtown Cemetery

The wind blows, a bell rings,
Another angel has his wings.

Every time you hear a bell ring, it means that some angel's just got his wings.

Essentially, a couplet made from a line in *It's a Wonderful Life* (1946), although it could well predate that movie as a folk-saying. *Wikipedia*: "*It's a Wonderful Life* is an American Christmas drama film produced and directed by Frank Capra that was based on the short story, 'The Greatest Gift,' written by Philip Van Doren Stern in 1939 and privately published by the author in 1945."

Robert Gielish (1933-1983)
Pleasant Hill Cemetery (Pleasant Hill)

The Winds of Fate

One ship drives east another drives west
With the selfsame winds that blow.
Tis the set of the sails
And not the gales
Which tells us the way to go.

Like the winds of the sea are the ways of fate,
As we voyage along through life:
Tis the set of a soul
That decides its goal
And not the calm or the strife.

Ella Wheeler Wilcox (1850–1919) was an American writer and poet. *Wikipedia* says "her best-known work was *Poems of Passion*. Her most enduring work was 'Solitude,' which contains the lines: 'Laugh, and the world laughs with you; Weep, and you weep alone.'"

Anon
Joseph Cemetery

To lose the Earth you know, for greater knowing; to lose the life you have, for greater life; to leave the friends you loved, for greater loving; to find a land more kind than home, more large than Earth.

Thomas Wolfe's posthumous *You Can't Go Home Again* (1940); reportedly, the line comes from a 1937 short story. *Wikipedia* says succinctly that "Thomas Clayton Wolfe (1900-1938) was a major American novelist of the early 20th century. After Wolfe's death, his chief contemporary, William Faulkner, said that Wolfe may have had the best talent of their generation. He is considered North Carolina's most famous writer."

Elida (1877-1963) & Simon (1876-1958) Miller
Union Cemetery (Union)

Warm Summer Sun shine gently here;
Warm Southern Wind blow softly here;
Rain you must fall, Please fall light
For here my Sweetheart sleeps goodnight
goodnight, Dear heart, goodnight.

Warm summer sun,
    Shine kindly here,
Warm southern wind,
    Blow softly here.
Green sod above,
    Lie light, lie light.
Good night, dear heart,
    Good night, good night.

Robert Richardson (reputedly an Australian, but I threw him in here for the Mark Twain connection; it was either here or the British), "Annette." Mark Twain used the lines for the epitaph on his daughter, Olivia Susan Clemens' (1872-1896), gravestone.

George Juneman
Municipal/Galveston Cemeteries

Why weep ye then for them who having won
The bound of man's appointed years at last.
Life's blessings all enjoyed, life's labor done,
Weekly they gave their being up and went
To share the holy rest that waits a life well spent.

35

Why weep ye then for him, who, having run
The bound of man's appointed years, at last,
Life's blessings all enjoyed, life's labours done,
…[7 lines missing]
Cheerful he gave his being up, and went
To share the holy rest that waits a life well spent.

William Cullen Bryant, "The Old Man's Funeral," published in the *United States Literary Gazette* (1824). *Wikipedia*: "William Cullen Bryant (1794-1878) was an American romantic poet, journalist, and long-time editor of the *New York Evening Post*."

Anon
Turner Twin Oaks Cemetery

So let it be that when Thy
summons comes to join that
enumerable caravan,
that moves to that
misterious realm, not like
one scorned to his dungeon,
but smoothed and sustained
like one who wraps his
couch about him and lies
down to pleasant dreams.

So live, that when thy summons comes to join
The innumerable caravan which moves
To that mysterious realm, where each shall take
His chamber in the silent halls of death,
Thou go not, like the quarry-slave at night,
Scourged to his dungeon, but, sustained and soothed
By an unfaltering trust, approach thy grave
Like one who wraps the drapery of his couch
About him, and lies down to pleasant dreams.

William Cullen Bryant, "Thanatopsis" (1817). I'll confess to not quite understanding the particulars of this epitaph, but it seems warm enough in its broad embrace. Personalized renderings are not uncommon on tombstones, but these deviations are noticeable.

    Wikipdeia: "Due to the unusual quality of the verse and Bryant's age when the poem was first published in 1817 by the *North American Review*, Richard Henry Dana, Sr., then associate editor at the *Review*, initially doubted its authenticity, saying to another editor, 'No one, on this side of the Atlantic, is capable of writing such verses.'"

Robert (1910-1997) & Marie Baker (1914-1995)
Athena Cemetery

BRITISH ISLES AUTHORS

Abide with me • Fast falls the eventide

Abide with me, fast falls the even tide.
The darkness deepens; Lord with me abide.
When other helpers fail and comforts flee,
Help of the helpless, oh, abide with me.

Henry F. Lyte, "Abide with Me." *Rumfordministries.com*: "Henry Francis Lyte (1793-1847), a Scottish Anglican clergyman, wrote a hymn entitled 'Abide With Me' that had eight verses in its original form."

Wikipedia: "Henry Francis Lyte was a Scottish Anglican divine and hymn-writer. He was born on a farm at Ednam, near Kelso, Scotland. Lyte's father was described as a 'ne-er do-well more interested in fishing and shooting than in facing up to his family responsibilities.' He deserted the family shortly after making arrangements for his two oldest sons to attend Portora Royal School in Enniskillen, County Fermanagh; and Anna moved to London, where both she and her youngest son died.

"The headmaster at Portora, Dr. Robert Burrowes, recognized Henry Lyte's ability, paid the boy's fees, and 'welcomed him into his own family during the holidays.' Lyte was effectively an adopted son."

Lyte's name is frequently spelled "Lyle," though from where the dispute arises I'm uninformed.

Mary Schultz (1922-1956)
Bandon Lodge #133 IOOF Cemetery

At the going down of the sun and In the morning we will remember them

Laurence Binyon, "For the Fallen" (1914). *Allpoetry.com*: "This is one of the most famous and enduring war poems, and it was written at an historic moment… just after the retreat from Mons and the victory of the Marne.

"As to how it came to be written, Laurence Binyon, who celebrated his 70th anniversary on 10 August 1939, says: 'I can't recall the exact date beyond that it was shortly after the retreat. I was set down, out of doors, on a cliff in Polzeath, Cornwall. The stanza 'They Shall Grow Not Old' was written first and dictated the rhythmical movement of the whole poem.'"

Continuing on, *allpoetry.com* notes, "Robert Laurence Binyon (1869-1943) was born in Lancaster, the son of a clergyman, and educated at St. Paul's School and Trinity College, London, where he won the Newdigate Prize for Poetry. From Oxford, Binyon went in 1893 to work in the British Museum's Department of Printed Books, before transferring two years later to the Department of Prints and Drawings where he eventually became Keeper and an authority on Oriental Art. His book, *Painting in the Far East* (1908), was the first book on the subject to be written in any European language. Binyon was also an expert on Japanese and Chinese Art."

Jermaine (1936-2002) & Walter (1937-1989) Murray
Tenmile United Methodist Cemetery

Bid me love and I will give A loving heart to thee

Robert Herrick (1591-1674), "To Anthea Who May Command Him Anything." *Wikipedia*: "Robert Herrick (baptized 24 August 1591-d. 1674) was a 17th-century English poet. Herrick was a bachelor all his life and many of the women he names in his poems are thought to be fictional."

Jane Smith (d. 2003)
River View Cemetery

Crossing the Bar

Sunset and evening star
And one clear call for me.
But such a tide as moving seems asleep
And may there be no moaning of the bar
When I put out to sleep.

Too full for sound and foam
When that which drew from out the
Boundless deep
Turns home again.

Twilight and evening bell
And after that the dark!
And may there be no sadness of farewell
When I embark.

For tho from out our bourne of time
And place
The flood may bear me far,
I hope to see my pilot face to face
When I have crossed the bar.

Crossing the Bar

Sunset and evening star,
And one clear call for me!
And may there be no moaning of the bar,
When I put out to sea,
But such a tide as moving seems asleep,
Too full for sound and foam,
When that which drew from out the boundless deep
Turns again home.

Twilight and evening bell,
And after that the dark!

And may there be no sadness of farewell,
When I embark;
For tho' from out our bourne of Time and Place
The flood may bear me far,
I hope to see my Pilot face to face
When I have crost the bar.

Lord Alfred Tennyson. *Wikipedia*: "Alfred Tennyson, 1st Baron Tennyson, FRS (1809-1892) was Poet Laureate of the United Kingdom during much of Queen Victoria's reign and remains one of the most popular poets in the English language. Tennyson excelled at penning short lyrics."

This poem is seen often enough to qualify as a palliative.

Carol "Ken" Davidson Jr. (1926-1979)
Lone Oak Cemetery

God's finger touched him and he slept.

Lord Alfred Tennyson, "In Memoriam A.H.H." *Wikipedia*: "'In Memoriam A.H.H.,' was completed in 1849. It is a requiem for the poet's Cambridge friend, Arthur Henry Hallam, who died suddenly of a cerebral haemorrhage in Vienna in 1833."

Lordalfedtennyson.com: "Fragmentary Notes of Tennyson's Talk," Arthur Coleridge: "One day we visited the grave of Lord Tennyson's shepherd; he died at the age of ninety-one. On his death-bed, Hallam asked him if he would remember in his will his [Tennyson's] two sons in Australia who had entirely ignored and neglected him. 'No,' he said firmly; and he left his 17s. 6d. a year to the poorest man in the parish of Freshwater. On his tombstone are engraved the Laureate's own words from 'In Memoriam'":

"God's finger touched him and he slept."

Wirt Kyser (1883-1902)
Knights of Pythias Cemetery (Rainier)

Do not go gentle into that good night

Dylan Thomas poem of same name. *Wikipedia*: "Dylan Marlais Thomas (1914 -1953) was a Welsh poet. In addition to poetry, he wrote short stories and scripts and the 'play for voices,' *Under Milk Wood*."

Wikipedia notes Thomas as "one of the most important Welsh poets of the 20th century," which leaves one wondering what other 20th century Welsh poets are we talking about? There are others? Arguably, his most endearing work is *A Child's Christmas in Wales*. *Under Milk Wood* was finished by the author backstage while the actors were performing it. He had, perhaps, an unwarranted confidence in his ability to handle alcohol.

Lee Read (1908-1973)
Antioch Cemetery

Full many a flower is born to blush unseen
And waste its sweetness on the desert air

Thomas Gray, "Elegy Written in A Country Church-Yard." *Wikipedia*: "Thomas Gray (1716-1771) was an English poet, letter-writer, classical scholar, and professor at Cambridge University. He was the fifth of twelve children and the only child of Philip and Dorothy Gray to survive infancy. He lived with his mother after she left his abusive father. He was educated at Eton College where his uncle was one of the masters. He recalled his schooldays as a time of great happiness, as is evident in his *Ode on a Distant Prospect of Eton College*. Gray was a delicate and scholarly boy who spent his time reading and avoiding athletics."

Victoria de Garcia (1946-1997)
Saint Matthew Catholic Cemetery

God hath his mysteries of grace
Ways that we cannot tell.
He hides them deep like the silent sleep
Of him we loved so well

God hath his mysteries of grace,
Ways that we cannot tell,
He hides them deep, like the secret sleep
Of him he loved so well.

Cecil Frances Alexander (1818-1895), Irish poet, "The Burial of Moses" (l. 77-80). *Wikipedia*: "Cecil Frances Humphreys Alexander (1818-1895) was an Irish hymn-writer and poet. Her 'Burial of Moses' appeared anonymously in *Dublin University Magazine* (1856) causing Tennyson to profess it one of the few poems of a living author he wished he had written."

Thomas Burgess (1858-1897)
Arlington Cemetery

He hath awakened from the dream of life

Percy Bysshe Shelley, "Adonais: An Elegy on the Death of John Keats" (1821). *Wikipedia*: "Percy Bysshe Shelley (1792-1822) was one of the major English Romantic poets and is critically regarded as among the finest lyric poets in the English language. Shelley was famous for his association with John Keats and Lord Byron. The novelist Mary Shelley (née Godwin) was his second wife."

Kyle Rowell (1980-2000)
Danish Cemetery

Home is the hunter
` *Home from the hills*
Home is the sailor
Home from the sea

There are a couple of options of where the epitaph comes from:

Home is the sailor, home from the sea,
And the hunter home from the hill.

Robert Louis Stevenson, "Requiem." Stevenson (1850-1894), the hugely famous Scottish author was a novelist, poet, essayist, and travel writer. His most famous works include *Treasure Island, Kidnapped,* and *Strange Case of Dr Jekyll and Mr Hyde.* Stevenson is beloved in Oregon for writing an essay on the Clackamas River.

A. E. Houseman provides the second option:

Home is the sailor from the sea,
The hunter from the hill.

A. E. Houseman (1859-1936), "Home Is the Sailor." Alfred Edward Housman was an English classical scholar and poet, best known to the general public for his cycle of poems, *A Shropshire Lad.*

Nils Olson (1917-1973)
Ilwaco Cemetery

Horseman
Pass by

Cast a cold eye
On life, on death.
Horseman, pass by!

W. B. Yeats, "Under Ben Bulben," one of his final poems, the last lines of which are his epitaph. *Wikipedia:* "William Butler Yeats (1865-1939) was an Irish poet and playwright and one of the foremost figures of 20th century literature. A pillar of both the Irish and British literary establishments, in his later years he served as an Irish Senator for two terms. Yeats was a driving force behind the Irish Literary Revival and, along with Lady Gregory, Edward Martyn, and others, founded the Abbey Theatre where he served as its chief during its early years. In 1923 he was awarded the Nobel Prize in Literature as the first Irishman so honoured."
   Horseman Pass By is also title of the first novel by Larry McMurtry.

Frederick Staver (1911-2002)
Willamette National Cemetery

Mad as the mist and snow

Bolt and bar the shutter,
For the foul winds blow:
Our minds are at their best this night,
And I seem to know
That everything outside us is
Mad as the mist and snow.

W. B. Yeats poem of same name. I rather think Mr. McArthur got the best of the Yeats' epitaphs.

John McArthur (1945-1998)
Jones Cemetery

I see her in the dewy flower
I see her sweet and fair
I hear her in the tuneful birds
I hear her charm the air.

Robert Burns, "Of A' The Airts The Wind Can Blaw" (1788). *Robertburns.org*: "Written during a separation from Mrs. Burns in their honeymoon. Burns was preparing a home at Ellisland; Mrs. Burns was at Mossgiel-Lang."

Mary Hartley (1886-1886)
Hartley Cemetery

Love like the ocean
Is vast and forever
And sorrow but a shadow
That moves over the sea

I found one attribution to John Gray (1866-1934) for this line, and I assume it's the English poet.

Anon
Saint Mary's Cemetery (Hood River)

My heart is in the highlands
My heart is not here
My heart is in the highlands
A-chasing the deer

Robert Burns (1759-1796), "My Heart's In the Highlands." Burns said of the song: "The first half-stanza of this song is old; the rest mine." This entire epitaph is from that half-stanza.

Wikipedia notes: "Robert Burns (also known as Rabbie Burns, Scotland's favourite son, the Ploughman Poet, Robden of Solway Firth, the Bard of Ayrshire and in Scotland as The Bard) was a Scottish poet and a lyricist. He is widely regarded as the national poet of Scotland and is celebrated worldwide. He is the best known of the poets who have written in the Scots language, although much of his writing is also in English and a 'light' Scots dialect accessible to an audience beyond Scotland. He also wrote in standard English and in these his political or civil commentary is often at its most blunt."

Joe Stocker II
Arcade Cemetery

My heart is a

Lonely hunter
That hunts on a
Lonely hill.

William Sharp (writing as Fiona MacLeod), "The Lonely Hunter." *Harpreet-Khara*: "It inspired the title of the Carson McCullers novel, *The Heart is a Lonely Hunter*. It was published in 1896 in the book *From the Hills of Dream*, a collection of Macleod's Celtic-flavoured poetry."

    Wikipedia: "William Sharp (1855-1905) was a Scottish writer, of poetry and literary biography in particular, who from 1893 wrote also as Fiona MacLeod, a pseudonym kept almost secret during his lifetime."

Stephanie Tomminger
Belle Passi Cemetery

Never seek to tell thy love that never told can be
For the gentle wind ever moves silently, invisibly

Never seek to tell thy love
Love that never told can be;
For the gentle wind does move
Silently, invisibly.

William Blake, "Never Seek to Tell Thy Love." *Wikipedia*: "William Blake (1757-1827) was an English poet, painter, and printmaker. Largely unrecognized during his lifetime, Blake is now considered a seminal figure in the history of both the poetry and visual arts of the Romantic Age. His prophetic poetry has been said to form 'what is in proportion to its merits the least read body of poetry in the English language.' His visual artistry has led one contemporary art critic to proclaim him 'far and away the greatest artist Britain has ever produced.'" Which is debatable.

Dick Margie (b. 1949)
Ocean View Cemetery

The widest land
Doom takes to part us,
Leaves thy heart in mine
With pulses that beat double.
E. B. B.

Elizabeth Barrett Browning, *Sonnets from the Portuguese VI*. *Wikipedia*: "Elizabeth Barrett Browning (1806-1861) was one of the most prominent poets of the Victorian era. Her poetry was widely popular in both England and the United States during her lifetime."

Martin Plamondon II (1945-2004)
Saint Johns Catholic Cemetery

Sacred to the

memory of
Cornelius DeBauw
Drowned Aug. 5, 1897
in Willamette River
While trying to rescue
little Peter Younker

Who farther seek his
merits to disclose

Cornelius DeBauw (d. 1897)
Sacred Heart Cemetery (Lake Oswego)

No farther seek his merits to disclose,
Or draw his frailties from their dread abode,
(There they alike in trembling hope repose)
The bosom of his Father and his God.

The last stanza of "Elegy Written in a Country Church-Yard" by Thomas Gray. See "Full many a flower" above for more about Mr. Gray.

Will ye no come back again

Traditional Scottish song, "Will Ye No Come Back Again?"
Rampantscotland.com: "After the defeat of Bonnie Prince Charlie at Culloden and his escape back to France, with the aid of Flora MacDonald, there were still many who hoped that he would return someday. 'Will Ye No Come Back Again?' is a song about that sentiment, written by Carolina Oliphant (Lady Nairne) in the first half of the 19th century. There are a number of versions of this song."

Ferguson
Miller Cemetery

THE BARD

Fear no more the heat o' the sun,
Nor the furious winter rages;
Thou thy worldly task hast done,
Home art gone, and ta'en thy wages;
Golden lads and girls all must
As chimney-sweepers, come to dust.

Cymbeline

Irma Hummasti (1911-1982)
Svensen Pioneer Cemetery

44

Good night, sweet prince,
And flights of angels sing
thee to thy rest!
Shakespeare

Hamlet

Samuel Goodman (1890-1984)
Neveh Zedek Cemetery

He was a man, take him for all in all,
I shall not look upon his like again.

Hamlet

David Baum (1922-1977)
Hillcrest-Hillcrest East Cemetery

This above all: to thine own self be true.

Hamlet

Sheila Box-Lee (1936-2006)
Stevenson Cemetery

His life was gentle, and the elements
So mix'd in him that nature might stand up
And say to all the world, "This was a man."

Julius Cæsar
Act V. Scene V., lines 81-83

William Swain (1914-1998)
Bonney Cemetery

I am constant as the northern star,
Of whose true-fixed and resting quality,
There is no fellow in the firmament.
Shakespeare

Julius Caesar

Thomas Allen (1884-1964)
Grandview Cemetery

I pray thee cease thy counsel

Much Ado About Nothing

Act 5, Scene 1:

Antonio:
> If you go on thus, you will kill yourself,
> And 'tis not wisdom thus to second grief
> Against yourself.

Leonato:
> I pray thee, cease thy counsel,...

Charles Reynold (1867-1914)
Zion Memorial Cemetery

...and, when he shall die,
take him and cut him out
in little stars
and he will make the face
of heaven so fine
that all the world will be
in love with the night
and pay no worship
to the garish sun.

Romeo & Juliet

Jason Hatfield (1975-2003)
Lone Fir Cemetery (Portland)

we are
such stuff
as dreams are made on

The Tempest

Henry S. Kranzler (1920-1999)
Scenic Hills Memorial Park

TRANSLATIONS

And she said in soft simple language
"When love truly enters the heart,
It will never be driven from it."

Is é dúirt sí os íseal i mbriathra soineannta sáimh
And she said in soft, simple language
Nuair a théann sé fán chroí cha scaoiltear as é go bráth.
When love enters the heart it will never be driven from it."

Captured from "comments' to a YouTube video of an Irish folk group, Clannad. I couldn't find its origins prior to that.

Isabeau Morse (1994-2000)
Saint James Cemetery

And this I know whether the one true light
kindle to love, or wrath consume me quite
One flash of it within the tavern caught
better than in the temple lost outright.

Omar Khayyám, *The Rubáiyát of Omar Khayyám*; translated by Edward FitzGerald.

Roy Powell (1910-1965)
Keno Cemetery

For what is it to die but to stand naked
in the wind and to melt into the sun?
And what is it to cease breathing, but to
free the breath from its restless tides, that
it may rise and expand and seek God
unencumbered?

Only when you drink from the river of
silence shall you indeed sing.
And when you have reached the mountain
top, then you shall begin to climb.
And when the earth shall claim your
limbs, then shall you truly dance.

Kahlil Gibran

Kahlil Gibran, "On Death," *The Prophet* (1923). *Wikipedia*: "Kahlil Gibran (1883-1931), sometimes spelled Khalil Gibran, was a Lebanese-American artist, poet, and writer. Born in the town of Bsharri in modern-day Lebanon (then part of Ottoman Mount Lebanon), as a young man he emigrated with his family to the United States where he studied art and began his literary career. In the Arab world, Gibran is regarded as a literary and political rebel. His Romantic style was at the heart of a renaissance in modern Arabic literature, especially prose poetry, breaking away from the classical school. In Lebanon, he is still celebrated as a literary hero. Gibran is the third best-selling poet of all time, behind Shakespeare and Lao-Tzu."

Carolyn (1936-1999) & Leslie Dehaven (1932-1989)
Oak Hill Cemetery

When you are sorrowful look again in your heart,

47

and you shall see that in truth you are weeping
for that which has been your delight.

Kahlil Gibran, "Joy and Sorrow ," *The Prophet* (1923).

Caitlin March (1981-2001)
Crown Hill Cemetery

You have walked among
us a spirit and your shadow
has been a light upon our faces

Kahlil Gibran, "The Coming of the Ship," *The Prophet* (1923).

Olivia Lewis (d. 2000)
Sunnyside Chimes Memorial Garden

Here with a loaf of bread beneath the bough,
A flask of wine, a book of verse -- and thou
Beside me singing in the Wilderness
And wilderness is paradise now [sic].

Omar Khayyám, *The Rubáiyát of Omar Khayyám,* "Quatrain XI" in his 1st edition (1859). *Wikipedia:* "*The Rubáiyát of Omar Khayyám* is the title that Edward FitzGerald (1809–1883) gave to his translation of a selection of poems, originally written in Persian and of which there are about a thousand, attributed to Omar Khayyám (1048–1131), a Persian poet, mathematician and astronomer. A *ruba'i* is a two-line stanza with two parts (or hemistichs) per line, hence the word *rubáiyát* (derived from the Arabic language root for 'four') meaning 'quatrains.'" The last word in the epitaph should read "enow." "Enow" is a cognate of "enough."

A word about meaning: *Wikipedia* elucidates, "The nature of a translation very much depends on what interpretation one places on Khayyám's philosophy. The fact that the *rubáiyát* are a collection of quatrains—and may be selected and rearranged subjectively to support one interpretation or another—has led to widely differing versions. Nicolas took the view that Khayyám himself clearly was a Sufi. Others have seen signs of mysticism, even atheism, or conversely devout and orthodox Islam. FitzGerald gave the *Rubáiyát* a distinct fatalistic spin, although it has been claimed that he softened the impact of Khayyám's nihilism and his preoccupation with the mortality and transience of all things. Even such a question as to whether Khayyám was pro- or anti-alcohol gives rise to more discussion than might at first glance have seemed plausible."

David & Althea Keyes
Lyle-Balch Cemetery

I expect to pass this way but once.
Any kindness I can show any fellow
creature, therefore, let me do it
now, for I shall not pass this way again.

Lucretius

Étienne de Grellet. *Wikiquotes*: "This, and variants of it, have been been widely circulated as a Quaker saying since at least 1869, and attributed to Grellet since at least 1893. W. Gurney Benham in *Benham's Book of Quotations, Proverbs, and Household Words* (1907) states that though sometimes attributed to others, 'there seems to be some authority in favor of Stephen Grellet being the author, but the passage does not appear in any of his printed works.' It appears to have been published as an anonymous proverb at least as early as 1859 when it appeared in *Household Words: A Weekly Journal*. It has also often become mis-attributed to the more famous Quaker, William Penn, as well as others including Mahatma Gandhi and Ralph Waldo Emerson." To which we can add Lucretius.

Wikiquotes continues: "Stephen Grellet (1773-1855) was a prominent Quaker missionary. Born Étienne de Grellet du Mabillier, son to a counsellor of King Louis XVI, at seventeen he entered the King's body-guard; during the French Revolution of 1792 he was sentenced to be executed, but escaped and eventually fled Europe to the United States in 1795, where in 1796 he joined the Religious Society of Friends."

Bernice Pearson (1915-1992)
Mount Union Cemetery

In the midst of Winter,
I finally learned
There there was in me
An invincible Summer.

Albert Camus, *Actuelles, chroniques 1944-1948*. *Wikipedia*: "Albert Camus (1913-1960) was a French *pied-noir* author, journalist, and philosopher. His views contributed to the rise of the philosophy known as absurdism. He wrote in his essay 'The Rebel' that his whole life was devoted to opposing the philosophy of nihilism while still delving deeply into individual freedom. Although often cited as a proponent of existentialism, the philosophy with which Camus was associated during his own lifetime, he rejected this particular label. In an interview in 1945, Camus rejected any ideological associations: 'No, I am not an existentialist. Sartre and I are always surprised to see our names linked....'"

Marie Tindall (1956-2007)
Oaklawn Memorial Park

Life is short we have not much
Time to gladden the hearts of
Those who travel the way with us
Be swift to love make haste to be kind

Wikipedia: "Henri Frédéric Amiel (1821-1881), was a Swiss philosopher, poet and critic. Born in Geneva in 1821, he was descended from a Huguenot family driven to Switzerland by the revocation of the Edict of Nantes." These epitaph lines are from his *Journal* (1868).

David Rupprecht (1947-1983)
Locke Cemetery

Look to this day!
For it is life, the very life of life,
In its brief course lie all the verities
And realities of your existence:
The bliss of growth, the glory of action,
The splendor of beauty.
For yesterday is but a dream,
And tomorrow is only a vision;
But today well lived makes every
Yesterday a dream of happiness
And like every tomorrow a vision of hope.
Look well, therefore, to this day.

Indian poet and dramatist, Kalidasa (which means "Kali's slave") lived sometime between the reign of Agnimitra, the second Shunga king (c. 170 BC), who was the hero of one of his dramas, and the Aihole inscription of AD 634 which praises Kalidasa's poetic skills. *Wikipedia* comments: "Kālidāsa was a renowned Classical Sanskrit writer, widely regarded as the greatest poet and dramatist in the Sanskrit language. His *floruit* cannot be dated with precision, but most likely falls within 4th Century AD."

Jones
Woodbine/Green Mountain Cemetery

Of things, some are in our power and others are not.
Epicieus [sic]

Epictetus, *Enchiridion*: "Of all existing things some are in our power, and others are not in our power." The translation is acceptable, the confusion of the authors is understandable.

Wikipedia: "Epictetus (55-135) was a Greek sage and Stoic philosopher. He was born a slave at Hierapolis, Phrygia (present day Pamukkale, Turkey), and lived in Rome until his banishment when he went to Nicopolis in northwestern Greece for the rest of his life. His teachings were written down and published by his pupil Arrian in his *Discourses*.

"Philosophy, Epictetus taught, is a way of life and not just a theoretical discipline. To Epictetus, all external events are determined by fate and are thus beyond our control; we should accept whatever happens calmly and dispassionately. However, individuals are responsible for their own actions, which they can examine and control through rigorous self-discipline.

"Suffering arises from trying to control what is uncontrollable, or from neglecting what is within our power. As part of the universal city that is the universe, it is our duty to care for all our fellow men. Those who follow these precepts will achieve happiness and peace of mind." My sentiments exactly.

Barbara Strayer (1963-1982)

To have placed the impossible word
on the rainbow's arc, then it
would have all been said.

Violette Leduc (1907-1972). Leora Skolkin-Smith at *readysteadybook.com* says, "Violette Leduc (first published in 1946) was often known as the 'most famous unknown writer in Paris.'"

    Wikipedia notes: "In 1955, Leduc was forced to remove part of her novel *Ravages* because of sexually explicit passages describing lesbianism. The censored part was eventually published as a separate novella, *Thérèse and Isabelle,* in 1966. Another novel, *Le Taxi,* caused controversy because of its depiction of incest between a brother and sister."

Joel Redon (1961-1995)
Spring Valley Presbyterian Cemetery

We shall remember that Earth cost us as much as ten
heavens.
Mandelstam

Mandelstam was a Russian-Jewish poet. *Wikipedia*: "Osip Emilyevich Mandelstam (1891-1938) was a Russian poet and essayist who lived in Russia during and after its revolution and the rise of the Soviet Union. He was one of the foremost members of the Acmeist school of poets. He was arrested by Joseph Stalin's government during the repression of the 1930s and sent into internal exile with his wife, Nadezhda. Given a reprieve of sorts, they moved to Voronezh in southwestern Russia. In 1938 Mandelstam was arrested again and sentenced to a camp in Siberia. He died that year at a transit camp."

Bethene Baldridge (1909-1993)
Union Cemetery (Union)

When you have tasted flight, you will
forever walk the earth with your eyes turned
skyward, for there you have been, and there
you will always long to return.
Leonardo da Vinci (1452-1519)

Presumably, Leonardo needs no introduction. Nevertheless, *Wikipedia* says this about him: "Leonardo di ser Piero da Vinci was an Italian Renaissance polymath: painter, sculptor, architect, musician, scientist, mathematician, engineer, inventor, anatomist, geologist, cartographer, botanist, and writer. His genius, perhaps more than that of any other figure, epitomized the Renaissance humanist ideal. Leonardo has often been described as the archetype of the Renaissance Man, a man of 'unquenchable curiosity' and 'feverishly inventive imagination.'" And he could draw.

    It's one thing to pay for having an epitaph's author engraved along with the epitaph, but to add his or her birth and death dates seems a generous gesture.

Yet sings, knowing that he hath wings.

Be like the bird in flight... pausing a while on boughs too slight, feels them give way beneath her, yet sings knowing yet, that she has wings.

Victor Hugo. *Wikipedia*: "Victor Marie Hugo (1802-1885) was a French poet, novelist, and dramatist who was the most well-known of all the French Romantic writers. In France, Hugo's literary fame comes first from his poetry but also rests upon his novels and his dramatic achievements. Among many volumes of poetry, *Les Contemplations* and *La Légende des siècles* stand particularly high in critical esteem. Outside France, his best-known works are the novels *Les Misérables* (1862) and *Notre-Dame de Paris* (1831; also known in English as *The Hunchback of Notre-Dame*)."

Patrick Moor (1943-1972)
Fairview Cemetery (Ontario)

Prayers

Deep peace of the running waves to you

James Codega (1947-2001)
Oysterville Cemetery

Deep peace of the Shining stars to you

Deep peace of the flowing air to you
Deep peace of the shining stars to you
Deep peace of the running waves to you
Deep peace of the quiet earth to you

A traditional Celtic/Druidic blessing that comes in a variety of wordings.

Michael House (b. 1948)
River View Cemetery (Portland)

Hail thou star of the ocean Portal of the sky Ever Virgin Mother Of the Lord most high.

Opening lines of "Ave Maris Stella," of uncertain origin and dating to at least the eighth century. *Wikipedia* notes: "*Ave Maris Stella* (Latin, 'Hail Star of the Sea') is a plainsong

Vespers hymn to Mary. It was especially popular in the Middle Ages and has been used by many composers as the basis of other compositions. The text is found in a ninth century manuscript in the Abbey of Saint Gall. The melody is found in the Irish plainsong *'Gabhaim Molta Bríde,'* a piece in praise of St. Bridget."

Thomas Thornton (1922-1997)
Saint Johns Cemetery (Barberton)

Hold onto what is good
Even if it is a handful of earth.

Hold onto what you believe
Even if it is a tree that stands by itself.

Hold onto what you must do
Even if it a long ways from here.

Hold onto life
Even if it seems easier to let go.

Hold onto my hand
Even if I have gone away from you.

Pueblo Blessing. The prayer gets repeated often, though sometimes attributed to the Hopi or Cherokee. The Cherokee themselves attribute it to the Pueblos.

Chaney
Canyon Hill Cemetery

Love God and find him within-
the only treasure worth finding
Meher Baba

One has to admit he had balls. According to *Wikipedia*: "Meher Baba (1894-1969), born Merwan Sheriar Irani, was an Indian mystic and spiritual master who declared publicly in 1954 that he was the Avatar of the age.

"From 10 July 1925 to the end of his life, Meher Baba maintained silence, communicating by means of an alphabet board or by unique hand gestures. With his *mandali* (circle of disciples), he spent long periods in seclusion, during which time he often fasted. He also traveled widely, held public gatherings, and engaged in works of charity with lepers, the poor, and the mentally ill." It must have worked, the world slowly gets better.

Paula MacMillan (1947-1995)
Mount Calvary Catholic Cemetery (Portland)

May the warm winds of heaven

Blow softly upon you and the
Sun rise with joy in your heart

Found listed only as "Indian Blessing." That would be American Indian.

Brownie & Lois Brown
Laurel Cemetery

O Son of Spirit!
Burst thy cage asunder, and even
as the phoenix of love soar into
the firmament of holiness, renounce
thyself and filled with the spirit
of mercy abide in the realm of
celestial sanctity.
Baha'i

Wikipedia: "The Bahá'í Faith is a monotheistic religion founded by Bahá'u'lláh in 19th-century Persia, emphasizing the spiritual unity of all humankind. There are an estimated five to six million Bahá'ís around the world in more than 200 countries and territories.

"In the Bahá'í Faith, religious history is seen to have unfolded through a series of divine messengers, each of whom established a religion that was suited to the needs of the time and the capacity of the people. These messengers have included Moses, Buddha, Jesus, Muhammad, and others. For Baha'is, the most recent messengers are the Báb and Bahá'u'lláh. In Bahá'í belief, each consecutive messenger prophesied of messengers to follow, and Bahá'u'lláh's life and teachings fulfilled the end-time promises of previous scriptures. Humanity is understood to be in a process of collective evolution, and the need of the present time is for the gradual establishment of peace, justice, and unity on a global scale.

"The word 'Bahá'í' is used either as an adjective to refer to the Bahá'í Faith or as a term for a follower of Bahá'u'lláh. The word is not a noun meaning the religion as a whole. It is derived from the Arabic Bahá, meaning 'glory' or 'splendour.' The term 'Bahaism' (or 'Baha'ism') has been used in the past, but the generally accepted name for the religion is the Bahá'í Faith."

Norman Edwards (1929-1994)
Pleasant Hill Cemetery (Pleasant Hill)

Oh God, guide me,
protect me,
make of me a shining lamp
and a brilliant star

Wikipedia: "`Abdu'l-Bahá (1844-1921), born `Abbás Effendí, was the eldest son of Bahá'u'lláh, the founder of the Bahá'í Faith. In 1892, `Abdu'l-Bahá was appointed in his father's will to be his successor and head of the Bahá'í Faith. `Abdu'l-Bahá was born in Tehran to an aristocratic family of the realm. At the age of eight his father was

54

imprisoned and the family's possessions were looted, leaving them in virtual poverty. Along with his father, `Abdu'l-Bahá was exiled to Baghdad where the family lived for nine years. In 1863, Bahá'u'lláh was again exiled to Constantinople. During the 1860s the family was banished from Constantinople to Adrianople and then finally to the penal colony of Acre, Palestine, when he was 24. During his youth he was 'shaped' by his father and was regarded as an outstanding member of the Bahá'í exile community. As a teenager he was his father's amanuensis and was regularly seen debating theological issues with the learned men of the area."

Should you want to know what an amanuensis is, *Wkikpedia* defines it as "a person employed to write or type what another dictates or to copy what has been written by another, and also refers to a person who signs a document on behalf of another under their authority."

Gracie (1903-1981) & Gilbert Melody (1904-1980)
Buck Hollow Cemetery

Where there was hate, she sowed love;
Where there was injury, pardon;
Where there was doubt, faith;
Where there was darkness, light;
Where there was sorrow, joy.

Lord, make me an instrument of your peace.
Where there is hatred, let me sow love.
Where there is injury, pardon.
Where there is doubt, faith.
Where there is despair, hope.
Where there is darkness, light.
Where there is sadness, joy.

Wikipedia: "'The Prayer of Saint Francis' is a Christian prayer attributed to the 13th-century saint, Francis of Assisi, although the prayer in its present form cannot be traced back further than 1912 when it was printed in France in a small spiritual magazine called *La Clochette* (*The Little Bell*) as an anonymous prayer, as demonstrated by Dr. Christian Renoux in 2001. The prayer has been known in the United States since 1949 when Cardinal Francis Spellman and Senator Albert W. Hawkes distributed millions of copies of the prayer during and just after World War II."

Phillipa Prather (1945-1997)
Lone Fir Cemetery (Portland)

CHILDREN'S AUTHORS

Goodnight stars, Goodnight air,
Goodnight noises everywhere

Margaret Wise Brown, *Goodnight Moon*, illustrated by Clement Hurd, first published in 1947. *Good Night Moon* needs no introduction to any American child. It is part of the canon of American children's literature and most children can recite it by heart. If not them, then most parents.

Fletcher McNeil (1998-1998)
Mount Pleasant Cemetery (Seattle)

I'm off to see the wizard

A case where attribution would be gilding the lily. I'm surprised the line doesn't show up more often. From, of course, *The Wonderful Wizard of Oz* (1900), L. Frank Baum. Needless-to-say, the mother (I presume) of Victoria more likely had the 1939 film, *The Wizard of Oz*, in mind when selecting this epitaph. Either way, she's not in Kansas anymore.

Victoria Gassner (1995-1998)
Restlawn Cemetery

Lord, the times we had together

Kenneth Grahame, *The Wind in the Willows*. About *Wind in the Willows*, *Wikipedia* says, "*The Wind in the Willows* is a classic of children's literature, first published in 1908. Alternately slow moving and fast paced, it focuses on four anthropomorphised animal characters in a pastoral version of England. The novel is notable for its mixture of mysticism, adventure, morality, and camaraderie and is celebrated for its evocation of the nature of the Thames valley." If read at the right age, it will never leave you.

Jeannie Kennedy (1932-1992)
Gethsemani Catholic Cemetery

THE NEW ENGLAND MAFIA

They managed to form a group all by themselves: abolitionists, temperance workers, educators, suffragettes, dieticians, writers, and a motley assortment of Transcendental philosophers. Together they planned to create a new America based on a curious mèlange of faith in the Lord and science. Ruling the 19th century, it was the last time our country was so influenced by an intellectual elite with a workable vision of a utopian future. In their way, they were nearly as important as the Founding Fathers. We will not see their like again.

> **Do not go where the path may lead,**
> **Go instead where there is no path**
> **And leave a trail.**
> **R. W. Emerson**

According to *wikiquote.org*: "Anonymous saying commonly attributed to Ralph Waldo Emerson, but apparently with no known source in his works or those of anyone else, according to *The Quote Verifier: Who Said What, Where, and When* (2006) by Ralph Keyes."

Should I stick a note on Elliot's tombstone?

Elliot Holden (1931-2002)
Havurah Shalom Cemetery

It is not length of life,
but depth of life.
Emerson

Emerson, apparently, did write these words. *Wikipedia*: "Ralph Waldo Emerson (1803-1882) was an American essayist, lecturer, and poet, who led the Transcendentalist movement of the mid-19th century. He was seen as a champion of individualism and a prescient critic of the countervailing pressures of society, and he disseminated his thoughts through dozens of published essays and more than 1,500 public lectures across the United States.

"Emerson gradually moved away from the religious and social beliefs of his contemporaries, formulating and expressing the philosophy of Transcendentalism in his 1836 essay, *Nature*."

David VanLith (1987-2005)
Valley View Cemetery (Vale)

What lies beyond us
And what lies before us
Are tiny matters compared to
What lies within us.
Ralph Waldo Emerson

What lies behind us
and what lies before
us are tiny matters
compared to what
lies within us.

Quoteinvestigator.com says, "Top expert Ralph Keyes wrote in the *Quote Verifier*: 'This quotation is especially beloved by coaches, valedictorians, eulogists, and Oprah Winfrey. It usually gets attributed to Ralph Waldo Emerson. No evidence can be found that Emerson said or wrote these words.'" That would be two out of three Emerson-attributed quotes are actually from someone else.

Robert Short (1910-1980)
Mount Jefferson Memorial Park

Nothing but the weary dust
is dead

For nothing but the weary dust lies dead.

Louisa May Alcott (1832-1888), "Transfiguration." Louisa was born in Pennsylvania, but moved to Boston at age six. "Transfiguration" was written as a memorial to her mother. *Wikipedia* notes: "Louisa May Alcott was an American novelist best known as author of the novel *Little Women* and its sequels, *Little Men* and *Jo's Boys*. Raised by her transcendentalist parents, Abigail May Alcott and Amos Bronson Alcott, in New England, she grew up among many of the well-known intellectuals of the day."

Louisamayalcott.org states: "At age 15, troubled by the poverty that plagued her family, she vowed: 'I will do something by and by. Don't care what, teach, sew, act, write, anything to help the family; and I'll be rich and famous and happy before I die, see if I won't!'"

Camilla Pillsbury (1863-1897)
River View Cemetery (Portland, OR)

Now twilight lets her curtain down
And pins it with a star.
Lydia Marie Child

It is also quoted in the following form:

Night dropped her sable curtain down, and
pinned it with a star.

McDonald Clarke. Unfortunately, Ms. Child, who was a biographer of Mr. Clarke, did not pen the above epitaph. *Wikipedia* notes: "McDonald Clarke (1798–1842) was a poet of some fame in New York City in the early part of the 19th century. He influenced and was eulogized by Walt Whitman and was widely known as 'the mad poet of Broadway,' a label with which he identified. He is, arguably, an early example of an outsider artist."

For her part, Ms Child (1802-1880) was an abolitionist, Indian rights fighter, and author of The *American Frugal Housewife*.

Kathleen Torrea (1907-1995)
Claggett Cemetery

The crown without the conflict

Harriet Beecher Stowe, *Uncle Tom's Cabin* (1852). *Wikipedia*: "*Uncle Tom's Cabin; or, Life Among the Lowly* is an anti-slavery novel by Connecticut author Harriet Beecher Stowe. The novel 'helped lay the groundwork for the Civil War,' according to Will Kaufman. The sentimental novel depicts the reality of slavery, while also asserting that Christian love can overcome something as destructive as enslavement of fellow human beings." As a young man, my sister and I went to a showing of *Uncle Tom's Cabin*, the movie, in Houghton, MI and were surprised to find it a silent movie. Yes, I'm that old. "Uncle Tom" is no longer a term of endearment. You'll note the age of the interred.

Logan Perry (1997-1999)
Finn Hill Cemetery

What the heart has once owned and had, it shall never lose.

Henry Ward Beecher. *Wikipedia*: "Henry Ward Beecher (1813-1887) was a prominent Congregationalist clergyman, social reformer, abolitionist, and speaker in the mid to late 19th century. An 1875 adultery trial in which he was accused of having an affair with a married woman was one of the most notorious American trials of the 19th century. Henry was especially close to his sister Harriet [Beecher Stowe, see above], two years his senior, according to the web site of the Plymouth Church in Brooklyn Heights, New York City. 'This friendship with Harriet continued throughout their lives, and she was still listed on the membership rolls of Plymouth Church when she died in 1896.'"

> Norman & Sharon Martin
> Cliffside Cemetery

SLOGANEERING

From the flames of Hell,
To the Gates of Glory,
Going home

Wildland Firefighter Foundation slogan. The origin of the slogan is not explained, but their mission statement includes: "Wildland Firefighter Foundation's main focus is to help families of firefighters killed in the line of duty and to assist injured firefighters and their families. We honor and acknowledge past, present, and future members of the wildland firefighting community."

> Richard Moore (1982-2003)
> Sandy Ridge Cemetery

God grant me the serenity to accept
The things I cannot change,
The courage to change the
Things I can,
And the wisdom to know the
Difference

Reinhold Niebuhr, "Serenity Prayer." Adopted by A.A. There are several versions of this out there and its authorship is in question. When pressed (according to *Wikipedia*) Niebuhr himself said, "'Of course, it may have been spooking around for years, even centuries, but I don't think so. I honestly do believe that I wrote it myself.'"

> E. W. Eldridge (1918-1987)
> Cliffside Cemetery

Let me win. But if I cannot win,
Let me be brave in the attempt.

Special Olympics motto. *Wikipedia*: "The first International Special Olympics Summer Games were held at Soldier Field in Chicago in 1968. Anne McGlone Burke, a physical education teacher with the Chicago Park District, began with the idea for a one-time Olympic-style athletic competition for people with special needs. Burke then approached Eunice Kennedy Shriver, head of the Joseph P. Kennedy, Jr. Foundation, to fund the event." Who penned the motto is unknown.

Thomas Haffner (1962-2000)
Cornelius United Methodist Cemetery

Novus ordo seclorum
A new world order for all ages

Wikipedia: "The phrase is also mis-translated as 'New World Order' by many people who believe in a conspiracy behind the design; however, it directly translates to 'New Order of the Ages.' It appears on the reverse side of the Great Seal of the United States."

Carl Halvorson (1916-1999)
River View Cemetery (Portland)

Silently slipped away across that
shadowy unknown sea. We have
no charts of their late voyage
with our love full of hope and faith
we too will sail o'er the unknown sea

From the "Memorial Service" section of the *Rainbow Girl's Bible*, published by Rev. W. Mark Sexson (1929).

Christie (b. 1947) & Roy (1940-1988) Hamilton
Evergreen Memorial Cemetery

Potpourri

Basic research is what I am doing
when I do not know what I am doing.
W. v.Braun

Wernher von Braun. *Wikipedia*: "Wernher Magnus Maximilian, Freiherr von Braun (1912-1977) was a German-born rocket scientist, aerospace engineer, space architect, and one of the leading figures in the development of rocket technology in Nazi Germany during World War II and, subsequently, the United States. In his 20s and early 30s, von Braun was the central figure in Germany's rocket development program, responsible for the design and realization of the V-2 combat rocket during World War II. After the war, he and some select members of his rocket team were taken to the United States as part of the then-secret Operation Paperclip."

All-in-all, a curious epitaph beginning with its non-sectarian humor that

60

seems a little lightweight for eternity, not to mention from a person of questionable ethics. Given the deceased's patronym, Germanic pride might come into play here.

Kirk (1938-1994) & Gerlind (b. 1936) Wuepper
Ocean View Cemetery

Hope sees a star, and listening love
Can hear the rustle of a wing.

Robert Green Ingersoll, "A Tribute to Ebon C. Ingersoll," Robert's brother. *Wikipedia*: "Robert Green 'Bob' Ingersoll (1833-1899) was a Civil War veteran, American political leader, and orator during the Golden Age of Freethought, noted for his broad range of culture and his defense of agnosticism. He was nicknamed 'The Great Agnostic.'" Today he might no longer equivocate.

I've found this epitaph twice, and it's shared with Woody Hayes.

David McKnight (1860-1948)
Sandridge Cemetery

If Roses Grow in Heaven

If roses grow in heaven
Lord please pick a bunch for me.
Place them in my baby's arms
And tell her they're from me.

Tell her I love her and miss her,
And when she turns to smile,
Place a kiss on her cheek,
And hold her for a while.

Because remembering her is easy,
I do it every day.
But there's an ache within my heart
That will never go away.

Author Unknown

I don't know how more romantic yet sad an entry there can be: Willow Waite in Moon Creek Cemetery? Really?

Willow Waite (2004-2005)
Moon Creek Cemetery

Laugh a little
Live a little

Try a little mirth
Sing a little
Bring a little
Happiness to Earth

Give a little, live a little, try a little mirth;
Sing a little, bring a little happiness to earth.

From *St. Dunstan's Red and White*; Chapter, "The Funny Man," pg. 61; no date. *St. Dunstan's Red and White* was the magazine of the St. Dunstan's University (Charlotte, Prince Edward Island) from 1909-1969.

Clyde (1927-2001) & E. Onitta (b. 1930) Barker
Bunker Hill Cemetery

Life is like a tree.
When a strong wind blows,
The tree must sway
Or be torn from its roots.
Chief Joseph

Chief Joseph. *Wikipedia*: "Hin-mah-too-yah-lat-kekt, Hinmatóowyalahtqit in Americanist orthography, popularly known as Chief Joseph or Young Joseph (1840-1904), succeeded his father, Tuekakas (Chief Joseph the Elder), as the leader of the Wal-lam-wat-kain (Wallowa) band of Nez Perce, a Native American tribe indigenous to the Wallowa Valley in what is today the State of Oregon in the Pacific Northwest region of the United States."

That sentence hardly describes the reverence in which the Chief is held here in the Northwest for his courageous attempt to lead his people to safety on a 1200-mile trek towards Canada and freedom and away from the U.S. Army, which ended shortly before the Canadian border. Aside from being a resourceful leader, he was an eloquent speaker who left us with the ringing, "I shall fight no more forever."

Jacob Hayward (1971-1998)
Multnomah Park Pioneer Cemetery

She was only home for a visit...
I did not look up when she walked in
but... held those moments of delicious
joy as long as I could before running
to her
From Cua Pead
An Autobiography

An enigma as much as anything else; one would think it would be traceable, but so far no luck. Neah Bay is a Native American community where Puget Sound empties into the Pacific.

Floyd Colfax (1920-1987)
Neah Bay Cemetery

Shed not for her the bitter tear,
Nor give the heart to vain regret;
'Tis but the casket that lies here,
The gem that filled it sparkles yet.

Belle Starr was buried on her ranch (1889) with a marble headstone on which was engraved a bell, her horse, a star, and this epitaph supposedly written by her daughter, Pearl. You'll note the date of Ms Cary's death. I don't have a photo of Cary's gravestone, so I don't know if it's from the time of her death or more modern. I suspect that the epitaph associated with Belle Starr was a chapbook poem and not an original of her daughter.

Orren Cary (1844-1874)
Franklin Butte Cemetery

Teachers are more than any other class the guardians of
civilization.
Bertrand Russell

Wikipedia: "Bertrand Arthur William Russell, 3rd Earl Russell, OM, FRS (1872-1970) was a British philosopher, logician, mathematician, historian, and social critic. At various points in his life, he considered himself a liberal, a socialist, and a pacifist; but he also admitted that he had never been any of these in any profound sense.

"Russell was a prominent anti-war activist; he championed anti-imperialism and went to prison for his pacifism during World War I. Later, he campaigned against Adolf Hitler, then criticised Stalinist totalitarianism, attacked the United States of America's involvement in the Vietnam War, and was an outspoken proponent of nuclear disarmament."

Rose (1914-2003) & Michael (1909-2002) Cassetto
Normal Hill Cemetery

The best and most beautiful things in the
world cannot be seen or even touched.
They must be felt with the heart.
Helen Keller

Hellen Keller. *Wikipedia*I "Helen Adams Keller (1880-1968) was an American author, political activist, and lecturer. She was the first deaf-blind person to earn a Bachelor of Arts degree. A prolific author, Keller was well-traveled and was outspoken in her anti-war convictions. A member of the Socialist Party of America and the Industrial Workers of the World, she campaigned for women's suffrage, labor rights, socialism, and other radical left causes."

Anon
Woodville Cemetery

There once was a twin brother named Bright
Who could travel much faster than light.
He departed one day, in a relative way,
And came home on the previous night.

This shows up in *The Oxford Book of American Quotations* as anonymously appearing in *Newsweek* for Feb. 3, 1958. As an epitaph choice, it is most unusual. He appears too young to have written it himself.

George Stringer (1949-1981)
Hilltop Memorial Cemetery (Nyssa)

Because the Bible Told Me So

There were many more biblical quotes to gather, had I been more inclined. I restricted myself to what caught my fancy. Anyone interested in folk studies should familiarize themself with the *Bible* as a cultural wellspring of many references. Selections are arranged as they appear in the *Bible*.

> **Great Spirit watch**
> **While we are absent**
> **One from the other**

Genesis 31:49

The LORD watch between me and thee, when we are absent one from another. [King James Version]

> James (1929-1997) & Patricia (b. 1931) Hamm
> Cascade Locks Cemetery

> **Let me go for the day breaketh**

Genesis 32:26

> Anon
> Turner Cemetery

> **May the soul be bound up with the souls of the living**

I Samuel 25:29

Part of the Jewish service for the dead.

> Barnard Kaplan (1929-2002)
> Kesser Israel Cemetery

> **My cup runneth over**

Psalms 23:5

> Bobby (1934-2002) & Ruby (1934-2000) Pruett
> Jefferson Cemetery

> **Wait on the Lord, Be of good courage**
> **and he shall strengthen thine heart**
> **Psalm 27:14**

Psalms 27:14

Minnie Burton (1936-2004)
Frank Abel Cemetery

Weeping may endure for a night
but joy comes in the morning

Psalms 30:5

Gladys Mayden (1912-2004)
Hobson-Whitney Cemetery

Mark the perfect man, and
Behold the upright. For the
End of that man is peace.

Psalms 37:37

James Wilbur (1811-1887) & Lucretia Stephens
(1812-1887)
Lee Mission Cemetery

The bird has
found a home
Ps. 84:3

Psalms 84:3

Barbara Flynn (1938-2008)
Redmond Memorial Cemetery (OR)

Oh sing to the Lord a new song
For he has done marvelous things!
His right hand and his holy arm
Have worked salvation for him.
Psalm 98:1

Psalms 98:1

Wes Epperly (1966-1985)
Yankton Community Fellowship Cemetery

I will lift mine eyes to the hills.
Psalm 121:1

Psalms 121:1

Edith (1900-1963) & Lawrence Reierson
Elsie Cemetery

May those who sow
in tears reap with
shouts of joy

Psalms 126:5

Catherine Browning (1957-1983)
Northwood Park Cemetery

So you thinketh in the heart, so it is

Proverbs 23:7
For as he thinketh in his heart, so is he

John Green (1929-1983)
Gales Creek Cemetery

She openeth her mouth
With wisdom and on her
Tongue is the law of
Kindness

Proverbs 31:26

Philip (1907-2003) & Eva (1913-19998) Lapidus
Havurah Shalom Cemetery

Founders of Northwood Park Cemetery   1977

Her children stand and bless her;
so does her husband.
He praises her with these words:
"There are many fine
women in the world, but you
are the best of them all."

Proverbs 31:28
Her children arise up, and call her blessed; her husband also, and he praiseth her. [The last three lines have been added.]

Donna Ellertson (1929-2002)
Northwood Park Cemetery

To every thing there is a
season, and a time to every
purpose under heaven

67

Ecclesiastes 3:1

Steve Zimmerman
Mountain View Cemetery (Centralia)

The sleep of a labouring man is sweet.
Ecclesiastes 5:12

Ecclesiates 5:12

Nona (1910-1999) & Emery (1908-1984) Headings
Fairview Mennonite Cemetery

For he seldom considers the years of his life
Because God keeps him occupied with the
Gladness of his heart.
Ecclesiastes 5:20

Ecclesiastes 5:20

Wayne (1921-2000) & Betty (b.1930) Roberts
Pleasant Hill Cemetery (Pleasant Hill)

"He brought me to the
Banqueting house, and his
Banner over me was love."
Canticle of Canticles 2:4

Canticle of Canticles 2:4
More commonly known as the *Book of Solomon: Song of Songs. Wikipedia*: "One
of three books of Solomon, contained in the Hebrew, the Greek, and the Christian *Can-*
on of the Scriptures. According to the general interpretation, the name signifies 'most
excellent, best song.' Some commentators regard it as a series or chain of songs."

Martin Propper (1935-2007)
Cooper Mountain Cemetery

All the waters cannot quench love,
Nor the floods drown it.

Song of Solomon 8:7

William (1942-1976) & Gayle (b. 1944) Raum
Glendale Memorial Cemetery

Set me as a seal upon thy heart,
As a seal upon they arm,

68

For love is strong as death
Song of Songs

Song of Songs 8:6

Sussman-Fields
Ahavai Shalom Cemetery

Having become perfect in a short while,
He reached the fullness of a long career;
For his soul was pleasing to the Lord.
Wisdom 4:13,14

Wisdom 4:13-14
  Wikipedia: "[*Wisdom*] is one of the seven Sapiential or wisdom books of the *Septuagint Old Testament*, which includes *Job, Psalms, Proverbs, Ecclesiastes, Song of Solomon (Song of Songs)*, and *Sirach*."

David Heller (1988-2005)
Columbia Memorial Cemetery

He shall gather
the lambs with
His arm, and
carry them in
His bosom.

Isaiah 40:11

Waldo Johnson (1904-1905)
Logan-Pleasant View Cemetery

They will soar high on wings like eagles. They
will run and not grow weary. They will
walk and not faint.
Isaiah 40:31

Isaiah 40:31

Steven Olds (1965-2002)
Elsie Cemetery

Fear not, for I have redeemed you.
I have called you by name; you are mine.
Isaiah 43:1

Isaiah 41:1

Stephen Russell (1950-2002)
69

For the mountains may depart and the hills be removed,
But my steadfast love shall not depart from you.
   Isaiah 54:10

Isaiah 54:10

Irene (1930-2002) & Leslie (b. 1925) Wright
Drain-Yoncalla Masonic Cemetery

Peace like unto a river

Isaiah 66:12
        For thus saith the Lord, Behold, I will extend peace to her like a river, and the glory of the Gentiles like a flowing stream: then shall ye suck, ye shall be borne upon her sides, and be dandled upon her knees.

Charles Beatie (1827-1882)
Carus Cemetery

Before I made you in your mother's
womb, I chose you
   Jeremiah 1:5

Jeremiah 1:5

Nigel Elsea
Mitchell Cemetery

Blessed are the merciful

Matthew 5:7

James Conrad (1919-1968)
Eureka Cemetery

Blessed are the peacemakers

Matthew 5:9

Carole Galer (1930-2001)
Hopewell Cemetery (Hopewell)

Jesus said, "Look at the birds of the air."

Matthew 6:26

James (b. 1926) & Maxine (1923-1996) Roherty

Sacred Heart Cemetery (Lake Oswego)

Whoever humbles himself like this child is the greatest in the kingdom of heaven.

Matthew 18:4

Dallas Dienhart III (1996-1999)
River View Cemetery (Portland)

*Watch therefore; for ye know not
what hour your Lord doth come.*

Matthew 24:42

Mattie Smith (1855-1896)
Kelly Cemetery

*Well done, good and faithful handmaiden.
Enter into the joy of the Lord.
Matthew 25:23*

Matthew 25:23

Juanita McGhee (1913-1998)
Fern Ridge Cemetery (Seal Rock)

*Out of the goodness of his heart
He helped the lame,
He invited the poor,
He gave to those who didn't have.
For now, He is waiting
For the Resurrection,
For his reward is in Heaven.
Amen
Luke 14:12-14*

Luke 14:12-14

Jerry Cummings (1958-2000)
Fern Hill Cemetery (Menlo, WA)

*Suffer little chil
dren to come unto
me and forbid
them not.*

Luke 18:16

Johnston (1900-1902)
Civil Bend Cemetery

Greater love hath no man than this,
That a man lay down his life for
His friends.

John 15:13

Willie Dowell (1891-1918)
Belvieu Cemetery

And your sorrow will then turn into joy.

John 16:20

Elisabeth Sarver
Bethel Lutheran Cemetery

But when the morning
had now come, Jesus
stood on the shore.
    John 21:4

John 21:4

Virginia Hillyard (1989-1994)
Amboy Cemetery

All things work together for good
for those who love the Lord and for those who
are called according to his plan.   Romans 8:25

Romans 8:25

Charles Coleman (1941-1983)
Pacific Sunset Cemetery

Love is patient. Love is kind. Love never fails.
Faith, hope and love remain, and the greatest of these is
    love.

I Corinthians 13
        Whence also: "When I was a child, I spoke as a child, I felt as a child, I thought as a child. Now that I have become a man, I have put away childish things."

72

Thomas (1944-2001) & Eva (b. 1961) Hunting
Mount Calvary Catholic Cemetery

Love bears all things.
Believes all things.
Hopes all things.
Endures all things.
Love never ends.

I Corinthians 13:7-8
Periods not in the original.

Sarah Short (1918-2005)
Mount Jefferson Memorial Park

and the greatest of all these is love

I Corinthians 13:13

June Alaspa (1919-2001)
Fern Prairie Cemetery

For we know
that if our earth-
ly house of this
tabernacle were
dissolved, we have
a building of God,
an house, not made
with hands eternal
in the heavens.
*   II Corinthians 5:1*

II Corinthians 5:1

Anon
Frank Abel Cemetery

To "an house not made with hands"

II Corinthians 5:1

Floyd McNett (1882-1956)
Forest Lawn Cemetery (Gresham)

I thank my God every time I remember you.

73

Philippians 1:3

Philippians 1:3

> Robert Allen (1966-2002)
> La Center Cemetery

He finished well.
Philippians 3:10

Philippians 3:10

> Dana Haynes (1950-2006)
> Brainard Cemetery

He is able to keep me from falling.

Jude 24

> Richard Schaeffer (1954-1985)
> Greenwood Cemetery (Cathlamet)

And God shall wipe away all tears
from their eyes; and there shall be
no more death, neither sorrow,
nor crying, neither shall there be
any more pain; for the former things
are passed away.

Revelations 21:4

> Anon
> Weston Cemetery

Too Loved To Be Forgotten
(Palliatives)

I began by calling these epitaphs "bromides," but that lent too pejorative an air to them. "Palliatives" seems more appropriate in that, while neither original nor altering reality in any sense, they sooth the mourner and express what may for them be difficult.

The first rule of palliatives is that they can't be written by the deceased or anyone connected to them. In fact, their authorship is usually unknown. Often as not, they're drawn from collections of sentimental verse which funeral parlors keep at the ready and have since time immemorial. Around the turn of the twentieth century here in the Territory, such chapbook poems were *de rigueur*; and most of the time, if anyone wrote anything extensive on their tombstone, it was a palliative. They have not disappeared. They, obviously, encapsulate some people's emotions and speak for silent voices. It would be unwise to dismiss them.

Because of the importance of date when assessing a palliative, I have arranged them by date of death (most often). Palliatives without dates are arranged alphabetically by first lines at the rear of this section.

An amiable farmer here lies at rest
As ever God with his image blessed.
The friend of man, the friend of truth,
The friend of age, the guide of youth

> Lorenzo Tracy (1826-1866)
> Viola Cemetery

O, let us think of all she said,
And all the kind advice she gave,
And let us do it now she's dead,
And sleeping in her lonely grave.

> Elizabeth Kirchem (1825-1866)
> Viola Cemetery

This youthful bud so young and fair;
Called hence by early doom:
Just came to show how sweet a flower
In paradise might bloom.

> Myrtie Wiltfong (1869-1872)
> Sandy Ridge Cemetery

Early plucked is early bliss

> Frederic Blakely (1873-1873)

Shed not for her the bitter tear,
Nor give the heart to vain regret;
'Tis but the casket that lies here,
The gem that fills it sparkles yet.

> Orren Cary (1844-1874)
> Franklin Butte Cemetery

Where immortal spirits reign
There we all shall meet again.

> John Sutherlin (d. 1874)
> Valley View Cemetery (Sutherlin)

Death but entombs the body; life the soul.

> Elizabeth Nicklin (1834-1875)
> Mountain View Memorial

Barton thou art gone, and thy loss we deeply feel. He
sleeps afar from childhood's home 'mid strangers graves
alone. Will strangers please keep this stone set up?

> Willam Jones (1853-1877)
> Coles Valley Cemetery

Our time on earth was short,
Our days on earth were few;
In the same cradle we were rocked,
And the same mothers breast we nurst.

> Mary (1876-1878) & Frank (1871-1878) Woodell
> Summerville Cemetery

Dearest children rest and sleep
While we wait, mourn and weep.

> Olive (1869-1880) & Alexander (1872-1880) Bartlett
> La Center Cemetery

We only know that thou hast gone,
* And the same returnless tide*
Which bore thee from us, still glides on,
* And we who mourn thee, with it glide.*

76

Michael Minahan (1845-1880)
Lone Fir Cemetery (Portland)

Lo! where the silent marble weeps
A friend, a wife, a mother sleeps:
A heart, within whose sacred cell
The peaceful virtues loved to dwell.

Mary Keller (1825-1881)
Lone Fir Cemetery (Portland)

And have you gone forever gone
*   and left us here to weep,*
Till we are called to follow thee and in
*   the grave to sleep?*
Yet since thou could'st no longer stay to
*   cheer us with thy love,*
We hope to meet with thee again in yon
*   bright world above.*

Joseph Bernardi (1830-1882)
Saint Barbaras Cemetery

Husband and children, I must leave you,
Leave — yes, leave you all alone;
But my blessed savior calls me —
Calls me to a heavenly home.

Serena Winn (1854-1882)
Helix Cemetery

One little angel more,
Singing with voice so sweet,
Flinging its crown of gold
Down at the savior's feet.

Claytie Ransom (1882-1882)
Mountain View Memorial Gardens

Weep not for little Stella
Her gentle spirit's fled
She sweetly sleeps in Jesus
Among the silent dead.

Stella Ransom (1880-1883)
Mountain View Memorial Gardens

Father in thy gracious keeping
Leave we now our dear son sleeping

> Thomas Littlehales (1809-1884)
> Forest View Cemetery

Gathered in a good old age to the
assembly of the righteous

> Alex Thompson (1803-1885)
> Lone Fir Cemetery (Portland)

As pants the hart for the water brooks,
* So pants my soul, Oh God for Thee.*
For Thee it thirsts, to Thee it looks,
* And longs the living God to see.*

> Augusta Fee (1855-1886)
> Normal Hill Cemetery

Dearest franky [?] how we've missed
you since you sleep beneath the sod.
Now we know you rest in heaven
With the angels and with God.

> James Dudley (1886-1886)
> Hartley Cemetery

My heart once heavy, now at rest;
My groans no more are heard.
My race is run, my grave you see,
Prepare for death and follow me.

> Sarah Stockman (1801-1887)
> Helix Cemetery

My wife, how fondly shall thy memory
Be enshrined within the chambers of my heart
Thy virtuous worth was only known to me,
And I can feel how sad it is to part.

> G. W. Prosser (1851-1887)
> Oswego Pioneer Cemetery

One more loved form has passed away
One more tired body gone to rest.

And hands that did life's duties
Are folded o're an honest breast.
A loving wife, sister, friend,
Whose simple smile may greet us never more
Yet weeping souls keep fresh this thought,
She is not dead, but gone before.

> Charlotte Smith (1816-1887)
> Island City Cemetery

She sleeps, she sleeps, and never more
Will her footsteps fall by the old home door,
Nor her voice be heard with it's [sic] loving tone
By the loved ones left 'round her own hearthstone.
She has gone, she has gone, to her home afar,
To the beautiful land, where the angels are.

> Sarah Bowles (1826-1888)
> Oswego Pioneer Cemetery

Mother, thou has from us flown,
To the regions far above.
We to thee erect this stone
Consecrated by our love.

> Mary Milliorn (1811-1889)
> Milliorn Cemetery

One less to love on earth
One more to meet in heaven

> Issac Newton Yerian (1870-1889)
> Mayger-Downing Community Church Cemetery

Safe on the bosom of thy God,
Sweet spirit rest thee now;
Even while with us thy presence trod,
His seal was on thy brow

> S. A. Scofield (1836-1889)
> Normal Hill Cemetery

Dear Mary,
Thou wilt sleep, but not forever;
* Jesus died and rose again;*
Soon He'll come in clouds of glory

Thou wilt rise with Him to reign.
Mother, then we hope to meet thee
  And to clasp thy loving hand,
Then we'll twine our arms around thee
  In that longed-for happy land.

Mary Averill (1850-1890)
Holy Trinity Catholic Cemetery

They loved her, Oh so fondly,
This little treasured one,
But the Savior in His wisdom
Hath gently called her home.

Emily French (1885-1890)
Jefferson Cemetery

You are not dead to us,
But as a bright star unseen,
We hold that you are ever near
Though death intrudes between.

Martha McNutt (1840-1890)
Cornelius United Methodist Cemetery

Budded on earth to bloom in heaven

Ina Arms (1891-1892)
Brookside Cemetery

This simple monument marks
  a father's bier,
And those he loved in life,
  in death are near.

H. M. Knapp (1829-1892)
Fishers Cemetery

Thy trials ended,
Thy rest is won

Walker Nickle (1830-1892)
Westside Cemetery

One by one earth's ties are broken,
As we see our love decay;

And the hopes so fondly cherished
Brighten but to pass away.

Thomas Hayden (1816-1893)
Alsea Cemetery

There's a beautiful region above the skyes
And I long to reach its shore.
For I know I shall find my treasure there,
The loved one gone before

Minnie Smith (1875-1893)
River View Cemetery

This tablet to a sister's love
  Is reared by kindred left;
Her soul in bliss is now above.
  Her friends on earth bereft.

Anzonette Foskett (1859-1894)
Antioch Cemetery

Gone like a flower
Of the blooming June;
Fading in a day.

Anon (1872-1896)
Workman Cemetery

No pain no grief, no anxious fear
Can reach our loved one sleeping here.

Arthur Knowles (1873-1896)
Lone Pine Cemetery (Wamic)

We shall gather at the river
With our gentle Nettie dear.
We will trust her with our Savior
While we mourn her deeply here.

Nettie Kellie (1880-1896)
Neer City Cemetery

Sweet flower transplanted
  to a clime,
Where never comes the

blight of time.

Charlie Davis (1890-1898)
Comstock Cemetery

We can not tell who next may fall
  Beneath thy chastening rod.
One must be first, but let us all
  Prepare to meet our God.

Thank God, Mother Nature carries no "chastening rod." I get to skate on this one.

Helen Crowe (1857-1898)
Eyman Cemetery

The eternal judge of
all the earth,
Is just in all his ways,
Alike in those which
give us birth,
And those which end
our days

Helen Freed (1867-1899)
Lone Fir Cemetery (Portland)

Tis hard to break the tender cord
  When love has found the heart.
Tis hard so hard to speak the words,
  "We must forever part."

Henry Overholt (1861-1899)
Monument Cemetery

Kind angels watch her sleeping dust
  Till Jesus comes to raise the just
Then may she wake in sweet surprise
  And by her Savior's image rise.

Frances Kellendonk (1851-1900)
Underwood Chris-Zada Cemetery

Call not back the dear departed,
Anchored safe where storms are o'er,
On the border land we left them,
Soon to meet and part no more.

82

Henry Mounts (1832-1901)
Franklin Cemetery

Beneath the smoldering earth here lies
In peaceful silence low
The loving remains of parents dear
Departed from this vale of woe
Fond hearts so dear remind us
That faith the grave o're leaps
And when life's short years are past
In our celestial home we'll meet

School VanDeHey (1835-1903)
Visitation Cemetery

Peace be thy
silent slumber.
Peaceful, in thy
grave so low:
thou no more will
join our number.
Thou no more our
sorrows know.

Jacob Johnson (1851-1901)
Noble Pioneer Cemetery

How much of light, how much
of joy,
Is buried with our darling boy.

This is a short version of the Franzen epitaph below.

Leander Lenderman (1901-1903)
Brainard Cemetey

Peaceful be thy silent slumber,
Peaceful in thy grave so low;
Thou no more will join our number
Thou no more our sorrows know.
Yet again we hope to meet thee
When the day of life has fled.
And in Heaven with joy to greet thee
Where no farewell tears are shed.

Mary Stockman (1842-1903)
Helix Cemetery

Oh Love I am so sad and lonely
Here without you upon the earth
That the fairest spot in its realms
are to me but as desert dearth

William Miracle (1859-1905)
Eagle Valley Cemetery

The heart's keen anguish
only those can tell
Who've bid the dearest
and best farewell.

Anna Winter (1831-1905)
Lone Fir Cemetery (Portland)

The light of her young life went down
As sinks behind the hill,
The glory of a setting star,
Clear, suddenly, and still.

Roxie McNurlen (1891-1905)
Pioneer Memorial Cemetery (Umatilla)

It was hard, indeed, to part with thee.
But Christ's strong arm supported me.

Nell Guild (1878-1906)
IOOF Memorial Cemetery (Woodland)

Thou art gone, little darling,
Sweet child of our love,
From earth's fairy strand
To bright mansions above.

Earl Ries (1901-1906)
Olex Cemetery

In your charity
Pray for the soul of
P. J. Flynn

P. J. Flynn (1851-1908)

Mount Calvary Catholic Cemetery

To you the child was
only lent. While
mortal it was thine.
The child, tho' dead, is
yet alive And lives
forever mine.

Narup (1885-1908)
Visitation Cemetery

Up to the City where falleth no night.
Gathering home: Gathering home:
Up where the Saviours [sic] own face is the light.
The dead ones are gathering home.

Etta Muirhead (1889-1908)
Dayton City Cemetery

In love he lived,
In peace he died,
His life was craved,
But God denied.

Jacob Jones (1859-1909)
Highland - Fellows Cemetery

She has gone from us.
Longer here she might stay
She reached a fairer regon [sic]
far away far away

Ida Tortora (1878-1909)
Locke Cemetery

Not lost, blest thought,
But gone before,
Where we shall meet
To part no more.

Louise Christkrautz (1855-1910)
Lake View Cemetery (Seattle)

Pearl thou hast gone and left us
Here the loss we deeply feel

85

But tis God that hath bereft us
He can all sorrows heal

> Pearl Coons (1890-1910)
> Idlewild Cemetery

Tis a little grave but oh have care,
For our fondest hopes lie buried there.
All our light all our joy,
Is buried with our darling boy.

> Franzen (1909-1910)
> Lyle-Balch Cemetery

Unseen he lingers with us still,
And Heavenward guides our weary feet.
His kindly words
    his smiles and deeds of love
Live in our memory
    where e'er we move
A spirit presence sweet.

> John Alspaugh (1882-1910)
> Foster Cemetery (Eagle Creek)

Dear Father, in earth's thorny paths,
    How long thy feet have trod,
To find at last this peaceful rest,
    Safe in the arms of God.

> Anthony Binder (1828-1911)
> Elkton Cemetery

We had a little treasure once
She was our joy and pride
We loved her ah perhaps to [sic] well
For soon she slept and died

> Audrey Mosier (1903-1913)
> Canyon City Cemetery

Dearest Mother thou has left us
For in happier climes to dwell
Though thy going has bereft us
We know that all with thee is well

Margaret Wells (1833-1920)
Fir Crest Cemetery

Dear father of love thou
art gone to thy rest.
Forever to bask mid the
joys of the blest.

T. J. Holmes (1852-1925)
Whon Cemetery (Texas)

"Old man" cried a fellow passing near,"
  "You are wasting your strength planting here.
Your journey will end with the ending day
  And never again will pass this way.
You have crossed the chasm deep and wide,
  Why plant a tee at eventide?"
    And the planter
  Raised his old grey head.

"Good friend, on the path I have come," he said,
  "There follows after me today
A youth whose feet will pass this way.
  He has not come to twilight dim.
Good friend, I am planting a tree for him."
                                Anonymous

Paul (b. 1928) & Myrtle (b. 1929) Hayes
Little Falls Cemetery (Vader)

The voice is mute, and still the heart
That loved us well and true.
Oh bitter was the trial to part
From one so dear as you.

You are not forgotten Loved one,
Nor will you ever be;
As long as life and memory last,
I will remember Thee

Wenzel Illk (1881-1934)
Mount Calvary Catholic Cemetery

The hours part us but they bring us together again.

John Sarver (b. 1950)
Bethel Lutheran Cemetery

There was an angel band in heaven, which
was not complete, that took our darling
Annette to fill the vacant seat.

Annette Roesselet (1892-1961)
Columbian Cemetery

A broken doll was sent to me from heaven up above,
A broken doll to have and hold, a broken doll to love.
God does send us varied things; he even sent his son;
Recall the passage in His prayer - thy will, Lord, will be
*   done.*
God could have sent a perfect doll, but our broken one was
*   blessed.*
It's strange how that which seemed so sad should be a joy
*   and fun.*
I thank God for the priceless gift, my broken doll my son.

Scott Berkey (1962-1968)
Zion Mennonite Cemetery

It's not the size of the man in the fight,
It's the size of the fight in the man.

Earnest Emerson (1907-1972)
Lone Oak Cemetery

He had true grit

Alfred Lewis (1899-1975)
Coos River Cemetery

I live for today.
Tomorrow I might
Not be here.

Philip Hadley (1953-1976)
Arlington Cemetery

Beyond the golden sunset
There's a land of lasting peace
That's filled with deep contentment
And a sense of sweet release

A land untouched by grief or care
Where none need feel alone
And in that lovely land beyond
We each shall find our own

> Kelly Slayton (1965-1983)

Though the body slumbers here
The soul is safe in heaven

> Beverly Swanson (d. 1985)
> Buxton Community Cemetery

Where there walks a logger
There walks a man

> Steven Benham (1954-1989)
> Providence Cemetery

When we count our blessings
We count our mother twice

> Alice Hall (1915-1990)
> Dallas Cemetery

Remember
No matter where you go, there you are

Reputedly, Confucius said it first, but it's often attributed to Buckaroo Banzai.

> Robert Sayer (1951-1991)
> Pleasant Hill Cemetery (Pleasant Hill)

I'm free
Don't grieve for me now, I'm free
I'm following the path God laid for me
I took His hand when I heard His call
I turned my back and left it all
I could not stay another day
To laugh, to live, to work or play
Tasks left undone must stay that way
I've found that peace at the close of the day
My parting has left a void. Fill it with remembered joy
A friendship shared, a laugh, a kiss
Oh, yes, these things too I will miss
Be not burdened with times of sorrow

I wish you the sunshine of tomorrow
My life's been full, I savored much
Good friends, good times, a loved one's touch
Perhaps my time seems all too brief
Don't lengthen it now with undo grief
Lift up your heart and share with me
God wanted me now, he set me free

Harold "Heck" (1932-1995) & Eathel "Snooks" (b. 1933) Cook
Mountain View Memorial

Do not stand at my grave and weep.
I am not there. I do not sleep.
I am a thousand winds that blow.
I am a diamond glint of snow.
I am the sunlight on ripened grain.
I am the gentle Autumn rain.
When you awake in the morning hush I am
  the swift, uplifting rush
Of quiet birds in circling flight.
I am the soft sunshine at night.
Do not stand by my grave and cry.
I am not there...
I did not die.

Christopher Schantin (1995-1997)
Saint Patrick's Historic Cemetery

Just another day in paradise

Donna Ceaser (1967-1998)
Columbian Cemetery

Weep, but briefly for our mother as she enters
into the Abhá Kingdom, for she shall possess a joy
and peace that is unattainable on God's earthly realm.
Rather, rejoice in her everlasting and total happiness,
for her eyes have seen her Lord.

The poem is a common nostrum. The "Abhá Kingdom," coming from the Bahá'í, is substituted for the more common "Kingdom of Heaven."

Lillie Willis (1941-1998)
Lone Fir Cemetery

> *A rainbow makes a promise that life is here to stay, that*
> *promise means there's more to life than what we know*
> *today.*

This seems to be a children's song of unsure origin.

> Deborah Spotts (1955-2001)
> Saint Boniface Cemetery

> *no farewell words were spoken*
> *no time to say goodbye*
> *you were gone before we knew it*
> *and only God knows why*

> Dianne (b. 1942) & Joe (1940-2001) Trask
> Crystal Lake Cemetery

"The Boy"

Mom and her son strolling down the street,
Passed a policeman walking his beat.
Mom says to her son, "See that man?
When you need help, he'll do all he can."

He'll protect you when things get too tough,
He'll save you when people get too rough.
He'll stop you from doing something bad.
He'll comfort you if you are alone and sad."

The young officer turned with a smile.
He said, "That's the best thing I've heard in awhile.
It's nice to know you feel that way,
Because we sure don't hear it everyday."

The boy passed the officer all the time before school.
He began to think being a cop would be cool,
"If I could wear that badge and have a gun,
Shooting up bad guys could be tons of fun."

The one day the boy thought and found,
That for days had not seen his friend around.
His mom said, "I've got bad news for you
Because there is something sad we must go do."

The boy wore a nice shirt and had his shoes tied,
While his mom told him his friend the officer had died
He left his friends, his family, his wife,
All just to protect his way of life.

The boy has now grown into a man,
And he is protecting us in the only way he can.
He passes a mom and young boy on the street,
While he is out walking his beat.

The little boy looked at the new officer in awe,
Like he was the neatest thing that he ever saw.
The young cop crouched down with a smile,
And said, "That's the best thing I've
Seen in awhile."

Among the noble sentiments, the lines "If I could wear that badge and have a gun,/ Shooting up bad guys could be tons of fun" concerns me somewhat.

Jason Hoerauf (1972-2001)
Lebanon Odd Fellows and Masonic Cemetery

Fisherman's Prayer

I pray that I may live to fish until my dying day, and
    when
It comes to my last cast, I then most humbly pray...
When in the Lord's great landing net and peacefully
    asleep,
That in His mercy, I be judged big enough to keep!

Gerald Endsley (1926-2002)
Sparlin Cemetery

God saw that she was tired
And a cure was not to be
So he put his arms around her
And whispered "come to me"

Wanda Lahmann (1946-2002)
Stipp Cemetery

She who would have beautiful
roses in her garden, must have
beautiful roses in her heart.

Were it not common, this would qualify as "advice."

> Dale Lindquist (1942-2002)
> Mount Calvary Catholic Cemetery

Surely Jesus loves fishermen, for he chose them for his own

> David (1962-2002) & Brenda (b. 1956) Dill
> Camas Cemetery

Cat prints on our hearts

A form of this is more often seen on pet memorials.

> Catherine Linder (1955-2003)
> Willamette National Cemetery

Don't tread on me

> Theodore Gold (1926-2003)
> Willamette National Cemetery

> *Think of how he must be wishing*
> *That we could know today,*
> *How nothing but our sadness*
> *Can really pass away.*

> *Think of him as living,*
> *In the hearts of those he loved,*
> *For nothing is ever lost*
> *And he is loved so much.*

A rare case of a known author for a palliative. It exists, as far as I can tell, only as a palliative. Last two stanzas of "His Journey's Just Begun" by Ellen Brenneman.

> Ty Smyres (1983-2003)
> Evergreen Memorial

> *For heavenly deeds of kindness,*
> *Where even angels fear to tread,*
> *For giving up your comfort,*
> *For how you mirror God's own heart*
> *And countless other things —*
> *You've earned the right to own with pride*
> *These special [earthly] angel wings!*

Joanne (1959-2004) & Daniel (b. 1959) Creamer
Hermiston Cemetery

He who dies with the most toys wins.

If there is any epitaph which typifies the change in palliative gesalt, it would be this one. They may have become secular, but not necessarily this callous. My sympathies to the friends and family of Mr. Niebling.

H. M. Niebling (1931-2006)
Forest Lawn Cemetery (Gresham)

God took her home, it was His will
But in our hearts she liveth still

Madelyn Morse (1972-2007)
Amboy Cemetery

Just when the caterpillar thought
the world was over, it became a butterfly

Susan Riffe (1950-2007)
Mountain View Cemetery (Ashland)

One's life is laid in the loom of time
To keep a pattern they do not see.
While the weavers work and shuttles fly
'Til the dawn of eternity.

The Loom Of Time

Man's life is laid in the loom of Time
To a pattern he does not see,
While the Weaver works and the shuttles fly
Till the doom of eternity.

James (1927-2001) & Deloris (1928-2007) Suomela
Ilwaco Cemetery

To one who bears the sweetest name
And adds luster to the same
Who shares my joys
Who cheers when sad
The greatest friend I ever had
Long life to her for there's no other
Can take the place of my dear mother

Marian Goodwin (1911-2007)

Frank Abel Cemetery

A little time on
earth she spent,
Till God for her
His angel sent.

Welma Meritt
Jefferson Cemetery

A precious one from me is gone.
A voice I loved is stilled.
A place is vacant in our home
Which never can be filled.
God in his wisdom has recalled
The boon his love has given
And though the body slumbers
Here, the soul is safe in heaven:
My loving wife Eva.   Oscar

Eva
Saint Mary's Cemetery (Hood River)

Although he sleeps his memory doth live
And cheering comfort to his mourners give.

Anon
Eagle Valley Cemetery

Another link is broken
  In our household band
But a chain is forming
  In a better land

Anon
Mount Zion Cemetery

Call not back the dear departed,
  Anchored safe where storms are o'er.
On the border land we left them
  Soon to meet and part no more.
When we leave this world of changes,
  When we leave this world of care,
We shall find our missing loved ones
  In our Father's mansion fair.

Anon
Tualatin Plains Presbyterian Cemetery

Dear is the spot where Christians sleep,
And sweet the strains that angels pour.
O, why should we in anguish weep?
They are not lost, but gone before.

Anon
Odd Fellows Cemetery (Myrtle Creek)

Dear Mother, in earth's thorny paths,
How long thy feet have trod,
To find at last this peaceful rest,
Safe in the arms of God.

Anon
Masonic - Lafayette #3 Cemetery

Death is but a
kind and welcome
servant, who un-
locks with noise-
less hand life's
flower-encircled
door to show us
those we love.

Anon
Frank Abel Cemetery

Death, thou art but another
birth,
Freeing the spirit from
the clogs of earth.

Anon
Frank Abel Cemetery

Ere sin could
Harm or sorrow fade,
Death came with friendly care,
The opening bud to Heaven conveyed,
And bade it blossom there.

Anon
Fort Stevens Cemetery

God took the strength of a mountain,
The majesty of a tree.
The warmth of a summer sun,
The calm of a quiet sea.
The generous soul of nature,
The comforting arm of night.
The wisdom of the ages,
The power of the eagle's flight.
Then God combined these qualities,
There was nothing more to add.
His masterpiece was now complete,
He lovingly called it, Dad.

What Makes a Dad

God took the strength of a mountain,
The majesty of a tree,
The warmth of a summer sun,
The calm of a quiet sea,
The generous soul of nature,
The comforting arm of night,
The wisdom of the ages,
The power of the eagle's flight,
The joy of a morning in spring,
The faith of a mustard seed,
The patience of eternity,
The depth of a family need,
Then God combined these qualities,
When there was nothing more to add,
He knew His masterpiece was complete,
And so,

He called it ... Dad

Pa
Wallowa Cemetery

Her life was like a half-blown rose,
Closed ere the shades of even:
Her death the dawn, the blushing hour,
That opes the gates to heaven

"Opes" is the preferred spelling in this instance.

Anon

97

Jefferson Cemetery

Her life was like
a snowflake which
leaves a mark but
not a stain.

Lulu
Pleasant Hill Cemetery (Pleasant Hill)

It's hard to break the tender
cord when love has bound the
heart, tis hard, so hard, to
speak the words; we must
forever part.

Dearest loved one we must
lay thee in the peaceful
grave's embrace, but thy
memory will be cherished
till we see thy heavenly
face.

Margaret Cummings
Pine Grove Cemetery (Peoria)

O, Brother, first to
* leave our band,*
Life's song as yet
* unsung,*
While gray hairs gather
* on our brows,*
Thou art forever
* young.*

Anon
Frank Abel Cemetery

She has wandered into an unknown land and left us
* dreaming,*
how very fair it needs must be since she lingers there.

Excerpt from a longer piece.

Anon

98

So when a little
angel departs we
who are left behind
must realize God
loves babies,
angels are hard
to find

> Anon
> La Center Cemetery

Sweet is the scene when virtue dies
When sinks a righteous soul to rest
How mildly beam the closing eyes
How gently heaves the expanding breast.

This appears in several similar variations. For example, "orphan's" can replace "expanding."

> Anon
> Union Cemetery (Union)

There are thoughts that never perish,
*   Bright, unfading through long years;*
So thy memory we cherish,
*   Shrined in hope, embalmed in tears.*

> Anon
> Athena Cemetery

These precious
children from us
are gone our hearts
are sad but God [sic]
Will be done

> Anon
> Lone Pine Cemetery (Wamic)

We miss thee from our home, Dear,
We miss thee from thy place.
A shadow o'er our life is cast,
We miss the sunshine of thy face.
We miss thy kind and willing hand,

Thy fond and earnest care.
Our home is dark without thee
We miss thee everywhere

> Anon
> Vernonia Pioneer Cemetery

We only know that they have gone,
And that the same relentless tide
Which bore them from us still glides on,
And we who mourn them with it glide.

> Anon
> Riverside Cemetery (Albany)

Where immortal spirits
  reign,
There we shall meet
  again.
Over in the summerland

> Anon
> Frank Abel Cemetery

Within these gates the
  rosebud peeping
Sad as it may seem to be
Lies our darling soundly
  sleeping
Through out all eternity

> Anon
> Jordan Valley Cemetery

You are not dead to us,
But as a bright star unseen,
We hold that you are ever near,
Though death intrudes between

> Anon
> Cornelius United Methodist Cemetery

BEFORE I GO
(ADVICE)

Some advice is philosophical, some is pointed. Some is given with a smile, some with stern admonition. Sometimes it's your mother or your father speaking. Sometimes it's the preacher or your best friend. It's always given with your best interests at heart and the slight longing to keep talking after one is in the grave. You can hear Mom as she's fading away: "One more thing…" I'd pay attention if I were you.

1869 missionary
Bishop of Oregon and Washington 1880
Bishop of Oregon 1906
Be ye doers of the word and not the hearts only

Episcopal, one presumes, as his wife is buried next to him.

Benjamin Morris (1819-1906)
Lone Fir Cemetery (Portland)

A bricklayer's art lives
Forever be at peace   Loyal

Loyal Hardin (1923-2002)
Willamette National Cemetery

A fathers [sic] faith, strength, and wisdom
Is the foundation that builds
His children's character

Fabian Mack (1922-2004)
Hillcrest-Hillcrest East Cemetery

A friend is a friend at all times

George Jackson (1898-1989)
Brainard Cemetery

A hundred years from now it will not matter how much money you had, the sort of house you lived in, or the kind of car you drove, but the world may be different because you were important in the life of a CHILD!

Nancy (b. 1934) & Walter (1916-2005) Behrens
Pacific View Memorial Gardens

A life well-lived
   is a gift to the future,
   a memory that time endears...
And the light of that life
   will shine in our hearts
   and brighten the world
   through the years.

Northern (1950-1985)
Crawfordsville Union Cemetery

A man is prisoner
of his past experiences

Anon
Dovre Lutheran Church

A road without love or friends
Leads nowhere.

John Hodgen (1912-1989)
Athena Cemetery

A teacher affects eternity
She can never tell where her
Influence stops

Alice Oblack (1948-2001)
Adams Cemetery

All will be well beyond the blue

Wendell Pynch (1941-1978)
Comstock Cemetery

And early death?
innocence is better
than a long life of
folly

Anon
Lone Fir Cemetery (Portland)

Any man can be a father, but it takes
someone special to be a dad.

Garry Monahan (1940-1985)
Springwater Cemetery

As a tree is known by
its leaves, so a life is
measured by the number
of people touched and not
by the length of years.

Jefferey Calderon
Mount Pleasant Cemetery (Seattle)

Ask, when appropriate
Aid, when appreciated

Ho Yee (1927-1969) & Yin Sang Yu (b. 1927)
Knox Butte Cemetery

Back from the tomb
no step has come.

Lucien (1844-1922)
Oswego Pioneer Cemetery

Be a hero in the strife

Alfred Rodriguez (1936-2001)
Mount Calvary Catholic Cemetery

Be brave

Gil Ogden (1916-2001)
Odd Fellows Cemetery (Dayton)

Be generous

Glenda Sano (1945-2003)
Smyrna Cemetery

Be happy   Sleep Sweet   Grandma Hee Haw   G.G.

Betty Drake (1920-2003)
Gilliland Cemetery

Be happy... The best is yet to come

A. Lorraine (1930-2006) & H. Leonard (b. 1928)
Hawthorne

103

Be like this sundial
Count only the sunny hours

> Anon
> Falls City Cemetery

Be ready

> Charles Davis (1925-2001)
> Willamette National Cemetery

Before you abuse mock and accuse be sure
You have walked a mile in your neighbors shoes

Punctuation be hanged; those commas and apostrophes are expensive.

> Steven Mix (1953-1973)
> Reedsport Masonic Cemetery

Behave yourself

> Bonnie (b. 1941) & F. Wayne (1940-2000) Benton
> Canyon Hill Cemetery

Bend and say you love me

> Leone Keil (1925-1991)
> Aurora Community Cemetery

Carry on[,] friends

> Angela Shaw (1977-2002)
> Cliffside Cemetery

Celebrate the earth and sky
Soar with the wind
Let your spirit fly

> Levi Baker (1979-1995)
> Confederated Tribes of Grand Ronde Cemetery

Come sit with us awhile and share our sorrow.
Though you weep, share the joyful memories too.
Look in your heart: In truth you mourn for that
which has been your delight,
For joy and sorrow are inseparable.

Puddy
Mount Pleasant Cemetery (Seattle, WA)

Dear Lord, help us to stop the grieving because
Doug is gone, and let us smile because he was here.

Douglas Flatt (1951-2003)
Condon Cemetery

Devoted mother, grandmother
Holocaust survivor and educator

Not to transmit an experience is to betray it.

Judith Meller (1930-2004)
Havurah Shalom Cemetery

Died by accidental shooting
Death is certain, the hour unseen

The last line of this also appears as an epitaph in Hillcrest-Hillcrest East Cemetery.

Salem Dixon (1838-1853)
Hobson-Whitney Cemetery

Do all the good you can
To all the people you can
In all the ways you can
As long as you ever can

Hazel Stevens (1898-1975)
Dora Cemetery

Don't drive faster than your guardian angel can fly

Wade (1944-2001) & Diane (b. 1951) Kinney
Springwater Cemetery

Don't frown on your fellow man
And peace over all the earth will span
A day may come when you'll be glad
And say "That fellow wasn't so bad."

Wirkkala
Peaceful Hill Cemetery (Naselle)

Enjoy your day

Jerry Franciscovich (1930-2005)
Evergreen Cemetery (Seaside)

Family, friends, & fine wine
"Just a simple country doctor"

John O'Hollaren (1922-1998)
Mount Calvary Catholic Cemetery

For every joy that passes
Something beautiful remains

Janelle Biggs (1984-1994)
North Palestine Cemetery

Forever trusting who we are and nothing else matters

Mark Moore (1975-2001)
Mount Zion Cemetery

Full throttle

I don't know if this is advice or descriptive.

Travis Hofenbredl (1988-2004)
Greencrest Memorial Park

God bless the ground!
I shall walk softly there
and learn by going where
I have to go.

Kenneth Adolph (1950-1975)
Fern Ridge Cemetery

God makes no mistakes

Gary Pullman (1960-2001)
Mountain View - Corbett Cemetery

Good citizens are the riches of a city

Unofficial motto of Portland; quote from C. E. S. Wood. "Charles Erskine Scott Wood was born in Erie, Pennsylvania on February 20, 1852 to William and Rose Mary Wood. He graduated from West Point Military Academy in 1874 and served as an army lieutenant. Wood fought in both the Nez Perce War in 1877 and the Bannock-Paiute War in 1878. It was in this capacity that he experienced the southeastern Oregon desert, described as a 'lean and stricken land,' that was to have a deep influence on him," ac-

Ernest Bonner (1932-2004)
Lone Fir Cemetery (Portland)

Grieve not nor speak of us with tears, but
Laugh and talk of us as if we were beside you

Evlyn (1915-1985) & Elton (1913-1985) Everhart
Adams Cemetery

Have fun

Homer & Enid Hooban
Canyon Hill Cemetery

Have one for me

Allen Plotnik (1939-2002)
Willamette National Cemetery

His motto through life and
last words to his children
was do right be honorable
and truthful

Jesse Looney (1802-1869)
Looney Cemetery

Humanity lives before the
vision of infinite knowledge
but from a state of
finite being

Edgar Smith (1919-2000)
Mayville Cemetery

I follow the
Rules of no man.

Delia Powers (1959-2003)
Norway Cemetery

If we could look inward,
Honor our minds,
Instead of hiding them
In every cause, we would be

Less absurd.

The wisest man will learn
To love his soul
For only in the essence
Is the whole

Let us hope we know
What life is worth
When the day comes that
We inherit the earth

> Thomas Dant (1935-1988)
> River View Cemetery (Portland)

If we deny love that is given to us,
If we refuse to give love
Because we fear the pain of loss,
Then our lives will be empty
Our loss greater.

> Walter Morrison (1968-1998)
> Woodville Cemetery

If you judge someone
You have no time to love them

> Janice Tuttle (1954-1993)
> Lone Oak Cemetery

It is what it is...

> Warren Jaeger (1944-2005)
> Antioch Cemetery

It takes eternity
To live life to the full

> Christina Saalfeld (1969-1981)
> Saint Louis Cemetery

It's never too late to save the world

> Lyn (1946-2006) & Chris (b. 1945) Surbaugh
> IOOF Cemetery (Coburg)

It's nice to be important but it's more important to be nice

> Emery Zidell (1918-1996)
> Ahavai Shalom Cemetery

It's the journey
Not the destination

> Nicholas Conaway (1951-2000)
> Pleasant Hill Cemetery (Pleasant Hill)

Joy in the journey

> Teryl Vance (1956-2004)
> Skyline Memorial

Keep your face to the sunshine
and you cannot see the shadows

> Wendy Hood (1977-1999)
> Lone Fir Cemetery (Portland)

Knocking on doors before entering is always a smart thing to do. This is not just for the privacy of the owner of the room, but also for the person who wants to enter. What if someone was creating a surprise for another person and "hid" in a room to prepare it, and the other one barged in? The surprise and fun would be ruined. God is preparing a room for me up in heaven. The door is shut now, but when it is time for my soul to move on, I will knock and discover a glorious surprise beyond description. Lord, thank you for surprises and the fun associated with them. I am faithfully sure that yours will be awesome beyond words... like they always are. Amen.

> Kara Zander (1978-2002)
> Evergreen Memorial Cemetery

Lead, follow or get out of the way

> David Baum (1922-1977)
> Hillcrest-Hillcrest East Cemetery

Life

I wish I could say exactly how I felt

About the hand of life I've been dealt
There are a great many things I wish I could change
And sometimes it all seems so very, very strange
I have my problems and everyone has theirs
But all of us can climb life's tough spiral stairs
Death is a fate that all of us share
So we had better live life and show that we care
Life is too short to just toss it away
Because all of us will reach that all faithful day
When life as we know it will exist no more
And that is the day that we will all gain lore

Elizabeth McGrath

> Elizabeth McGrath (1974-1990)
> Lewisville Cemetery

Life is a precious thing that
we have to fight to understand,
and love with all our heart,
and give ourselves grace as we
fight for that understanding.

> Kelly Sandy III (1944-2005)
> Mount Pleasant Cemetery (Seattle, WA)

Life is just a flight through time
A peaceful interlude, hopefully for us all,
As we struggle here on earth. Eventually
Our Creator will say - it's time we fly away
With me to a better place. Amen.
        AD

> Albert Dering (1937-1992)
> Bethany Presbyterian Cemetery

Life is just one lesson
in our continuation of forever

> Jack Goheen (1922-1995)
> Firhill Cemetery

Life is like a
game, except at
the end, there need

not be a loser.

> Joe (1917-1965) & Roy (1945-1977) Spanish
> Mountain View Cemetery (Walla Walla)

Life is not a journey to the grave with the intention of arriving safely, in a pretty well-preserved body, but rather to skid in broadside, thoroughly used up, totally worn out, and loudly proclaiming, "WOW, What a ride!"

On a laminated piece of paper affixed above a photo-ceramic of Kurtis.

> Jeremy Kurtis (1983-2003)
> Olney Cemetery

Listen to the stars blink

> Paul (1986-1998)
> Sandy Ridge Cemetery

Listen to the whisper of a dream within your heart

> Charalee Hickman (1975-1995)
> Valley View Cemetery (Silverton)

Listen to the wild...
It is calling you

> R. A. Gerity (1928-1998)
> Lone Pine Cemetery (Wamic)

Live a legacy
Leave a legacy

> Troy & Marilyn Thompson (1961-1998)
> Gibbs Cemetery

Live hard, die young & leave a beautiful memory

> Donnie Beck (1971-1989)
> Aumsville Cemetery

Look up, take courage, the angels are nearer than you
    think

> Darlene (1963-1997) & Kourtney (1988-1997) Benson
> Bunker Hill Cemetery

111

Love
laughter
& the ability to see
the sun through the haze
are the rewards of
a heart that beats
to the beauty
of life

> Naomi Loyer (1953-1996)
> Tualatin Plains Presbyterian Cemetery

Love, laugh, live

> Joshua Turner (1985-2004)
> Riddle Cemetery

Love one another as I have loved you

> George (1929-1999) & Emma (b. 1932) Schmid
> Washougal Memorial Cemetery

Mountain Man
Be a friend

> Gerald Condon (1925-1982)
> Mountain View Memorial

Never an adventure too great

> Pitkin
> Owyhee Cemetery

Never look back, always look forward
You can't live in the past

> June (b. 1925) & Darrell (1921-1991) Leavitt
> Westside Cemetery

Never regret something that made you smile

> Joel Meyer (1984-2005)
> Camp Polk Cemetery

Never slack down in a hard pull
  Arlie

112

Richard (b. 1934) & Gloria (b. 1932) Walker
Rock Point / Gold Hill IOOF Cemetery

Nobleness
Enkindleth
Nobleness

I think I understand what this means. I think. But what an unusual word.

Milton Church (1879-1927)
Applegate Pioneer Cemetery

Nothing compares 2 U SK8 forever

"Nothing compares to you" appears on a stone in Frank Abel Cemetery. This epitaph preserves the spelling of the Prince song, but adds the tag "SK8 forever." Shelby was sixteen when he died.

Shelby Hajek-Richey (1974-1990)
Logan-Pleasant View Cemetery

Nothing stupid

William Lamb
Sacred Heart Cemetery (Lake Oswego)

Now that we have said hello
Lets take a walk on the beach

George Bales (b. 1908)
American Legion Cemetery

Only the person who risks is free

Brian Goodrich (1954-1997)
Dallas Cemetery

Open your Hands
and Catch the
Freedom you have

Royal Newman (1982-1999)
Mountain View Cemetery (Oregon City)

Peace provides us with the opportunity to find a solution
for every existing problem.
A. D. L.

Armin (1928-2008) & Kim (b. 1954) Lehmann
Yachats Memorial Park

Perseverance still is king

Herman Goldberg (1924-1996)
Neveh Zedek Cemetery

Primum non nocere

"First do no harm," which is not the same as "First do good."

James Barnes (1929-2005)
Roseburg National Cemetery

Protect the Bull Run; Thanks for stopping by.

Virgil & Dianne
American Legion Cemetery (Manzanita)

Reinvent yourself

Donald Homan (1933-2000)
Willamette National Cemetery

Remember the good times

John (1916-2000) & Margaret (1922-1989) Marson
Adams Cemetery

Remember the moments of the past.
Look forward to the promise of the future.
But most of all celebrate the present,
for its preciousness.

Anon
City View Cemetery

She loved the Lord
She is with the Lord
How about you?

Lidia Johnson (1950-1999)
Crescent Grove Cemetery

Sit long, talk much, laugh often

On the edge a stone bench in Mountain View Cemetery (Centralia, WA) is written:
"Sit long—Talk much."

114

Stick with me kid and
I'll show you the world

Thomas Walworth (1916-1999)
Willamette National Cemetery

Success

To laugh often and love much
to win the respect of intelligent persons
and the affection of children
to hear the appreciation of honest critics
and endure the betrayal of false friends
to appreciate beauty, to find the best in others
to give one's self, to leave the world a bit better
whether by a healthy child, a garden patch
or a redeemed social condition
to have played and laughed with exultation
to know even one life has breathed easier
because you have lived.
This to have succeeded.

John (1938-1997) & Beth (b. 1941) Bollman
Dallas Cemetery

The artist must know suffering to
know and appreciate beauty and truth.
I am an artist; my life and the action of
living, my media; expression of love
for life, my creation; and intensity of
experience, the brush stroke and
fabric of that expression.
  So when I suffer it is only for
my own joy of being, and when I am
happy it is only because I was once sad.
                    H. R. A.

Herbert Amos (1946-1975)
Brown Cemetery (Beatty)

The first person

115

one must learn to love
is ones [sic] self

> Forrest Huffman (1942-2002)
> Lincoln Memorial Park

The grass and sky go on
forever; it is a good day to die.

> Sarah Gray (1914-1999)
> Mountain View Cemetery (View, WA)

The greatest pleasure in life is doing things that people
say you cannot do, and doing it with the people you
love

> Charles Wyatt (d. 1988)
> United Church of Christ Cemetery (Ten O'Clock
> Church)

The greatest use of life is to spend it for something that
will out last it.

[verso]

From death there comes a blooming. From stress grows
beauty. From the holocaust is born peace. From hurt there
grows forgiveness. From pain there comes wisdom. From
weeping there takes place cleansing. From tears grow the
seeds of joy.

> Douglas & Melinda Pollard
> Mountain View Cemetery (Oregon City)

The real Chief Seattle said, "There is no death, you just go
to another world."

> Anon
> American Legion Cemetery

The struggle for athletic perfection
is arduous. Only those with the greatest heart and
fortitude become world champions.

> Doyle Kenady (1948-1999)
> Fir Grove Cemetery

The world don't owe you, you owe the world

> Hardy Billington (1899-1974)
> Fir Crest Cemetery

There ain't a horse that can't be rode
Or a rider that can't be thrown

> Norman Balsey (1928-1994)
> Cliffside Cemetery

There are other worlds to sing in.

> Orrin (1934-2001) & Kathryn (b. 1934) Holt
> Fern Hill Cemetery (Raymond, WA)

There is always music among the trees

> Elsie Mahler (1912-1991)
> Lone Fir Cemetery (Portland)

There is no kitten too little to scratch

> Marian Dingman (1920-1994)
> Pleasant Hill Cemetery (Pleasant Hill)

There's no place that far

> Joseph Williams
> Mountain View Memorial

Things never stay the same
You either go ahead
Or you go behind

> Sally Jo (b. 1954) & R. John (1999-1946) Leavitt
> Westside Cemetery

This world is not conclusion
A sequel stands beyond
Invisible, as music
But positive as sound

> Robert Adolph (1926-1986)
> Fern Ridge Cemetery

Time does everything

Ethel (1898-1992) & Milt (1890-1977) Cain
Normal Hill Cemetery

Time is a precious gift, let us use it wisely

Albert Terry Jr. (1930-1978)
Jefferson Cemetery

To the biggest little man I know
But when you straddle a machine
To race along the sea
You should be prepared to die
When the machine dies under you.
   I hope he was.

H. Dean Hassen (1932-1969)
Deer Creek Cemetery

Toward a world without violence

Alfred Allina (1938-2005)
Northwood Park Cemetery

Treat others as you
Wish to be treated

John (1902-1990) & Dollie (1904-1951) Lamar
Fairview-Scappoose Cemetery

Venture beyond

Matthew Ben-Lesser (1927-2005)
Scenic Hills Memorial Park

Walk softly...
Dreams lie buried here

From an unidentified cemetery in Montana or Idaho, I have an epitaph for one Delbert Welch (1933-2002) that reads: "Step softly, there's a dream buried here."

Ronald Turpin (1933-2000)
Mount Pleasant Cemetery (Seattle, WA)

We are not called by God to do extraordinary things but
to do ordinary things with extraordinary love.

Duane (1939-2003) & Joyce (b. 1948) Kelson
Forest Lawn Cemetery (Gresham)

118

When death grins smile back

Ted Dawson (1916-2003)
Willamette National Cemetery

Wish not so much to live long as to live well.
Treasure the past.
Enjoy the present.
Embrace the future.
Pursue your dreams.
You are a star in the face of the sky.
With love and respect to our family and friends.

Daniel Leonard (b. 1952) & Eulalia (2003-1952)
Slowikowski
Mount Calvary Catholic Cemetery

With universal love
I help myself,
Others, and all life
As an infinite law.

Halvorson
River View Cemetery (Portland)

World peace through
peace is not an action.
It is not something that anyone,
Even nations, can "do." Instead
Peace is the result of actions and
Attitudes which each individual
Can think about and work on.

Sandra Raph (1977-1993)
Island City Cemetery

You will find poetry nowhere
unless you bring some with you

Jackie MacGregor (b. 1933) & Ken Holmes (b. 1926)
Oswego Pioneer Cemetery

119

"DON'T CODDLE ME INTO THE GRAVE. I'M GOING TO MARCH INTO IT. I'M A MAN, AFTER ALL."

COME AGAIN?
(ENIGMAS)

Everyone appreciates a good head-scratcher. Some enigmas are awkward, some are amusing, some are graceful. Each leaves the reader wondering, "What was she trying to say?" It's good to not know. Not all mysteries should be solved.

I want you to know that it was hard to transcribe these without making comments on each and every one.

1936 Fords forever

>Robert Kindopp (1930-2003)
>Willamette National Cemetery

A fine young man ahead of us on the trail

>Anon
>Lewis and Clark Cemetery

*A man
And his flags*

>Lawrence Olwell (1926-2002)
>Willamette National Cemetery

A man and his mountain

>Will Brown (1855-1936)
>Riddle Cemetery

*A woman is like the snow that falls upon the river,
White for a moment, and gone forever.*

>Nancy Lander (1868-1887)
>Canyon Hill Cemetery

*aka Elkhound
King of the Beardies*

>Arlan Caya (1939-1995)
>Mountain View Cemetery (Oregon City)

Always on the edge

>Mathew Blissit (1972-2001)
>Claggett Cemetery

And the thing
Of it is

> Robert Smalley Sr. (1924-2000)
> Willamette National Cemetery

Because that's my job

> Cathy Horton (1957-2004)
> Shaarie Torah Cemetery

Be wise and Fentonize

> Fenton Galer (b. 1929)
> Hopewell Cemetery (Hopewell)

Break, Air Duck

> Thomas Teel (1927-2002)
> Union Point Cemetery

Care authority

> Trudy Tyler (1949-2006)
> Rock Point/Gold Hill IOOF Cemetery

Don loved trains

> Don Funk
> Kelly Cemetery

Don't
slam the doors

Under an etching of a 1960s convertible. It could, I imagine, be filed under "Advice."

> Bill (1929-2001)
> Moon Creek Cemetery

Driving down old country roads

> Guy Gilliam (1937-2006)
> Highland Cemetery (Elgin)

Everything I do is in memory of my husband. The day I die
and go to heaven,
I will be leaving a wondrous gift for all my children.

I'll confess to being baffled by this epitaph; what gift is she alluding to? But it comes with a great photo.

> Domatila Tavera (1933-2009)
> Fern Hill Cemetery (Blooming)

Excuse me...

> Kay Shineflug (1939-1998)
> Eureka Cemetery (Newport)

Fell asleep

Perhaps this should have been categorized under "Humor" Or "Philosophical."

> Anon (d. 1877)
> Union Cemetery (Union)

Finished with engines

> Malcolm Rogers (1928-1990)
> Adams Cemetery

For what you have given me I'll be forever greatful [sic]. Therefore, please accept my gift to you, the sun, the stars, the mountains, the oceans and all the architecture of nature that will endure.

Who is speaking to whom?

> Juanita (b. 1915) & Clifford (1911-1995) Ramey
> Grandview Cemetery

God's Patriot

> Kermit Griffith (1931-2006)
> Eagle Point National Cemetery

Good ol' country sunshine

> Rene Martens (1909-1984)
> Upper Valley Cemetery

Got Jets!

Under an engraving of a pig adorned with a flowered collar and standing atop a golf tee.

Bruce Hayward (1952-1996)
Jacksonville Cemetery

Gregg was here

Gregory Sands (1952-1973)
Brush Prairie Cemetery

Have a day

Dick Ferris (1925-2002)
Willamette National Cemetery

*Have you heard
the one about*

Edwin Herzog
Eagle Point National Cemetery

He has awakened from the dream of life

Christopher O'Reilly (1956-1970)
Evergreen Cemetery (Tucson)

He looked at the stars

William Vargas (1955-2003)
Redmond Memorial Cemetery

*He loved his
Dog Loki*

John Crecelius (1936-2002)
Willamette National Cemetery

He wandered - he returned

John Elsberry (1907-1957)
Cross Cut Cemetery (Texas)

*Heaven sings
Capes & wings*

Gerald (1933-2002) & Mary (1936-2003) Soderberg
Willamette National Cemetery

Hero of a thousand faces

Karl Hurd (1930-2004)

124

Evergreen Cemetery (Seaside)

Horses forever

Marian (1943-2005) & Ray (b. 1937) Wood
Hilltop Cemetery

I am a little Hendu
I do as I can do
My little pants & shirt
Do not meet but my
Little skin do

This has all the feel of a children's nursery rhyme, but I can't find traces of it. At the very least, Brian's mother said this to him at night before he went to sleep or while taking a bath.

Brian "Hendu" Henderson (1963-1994)
Walker Community Church Cemetery

I can only imagine

Steven Weathers (1957-2005)
Antioch Cemetery

I love my garden in the morning

Marjorie Read (1914-2002)
Atioch Cemetery

I once had a girlfriend like that

William Druery
Odd Fellows Cemetery (Dayton)

I see dumb people

"I see dead people" became a catch-phrase after it appeared in the 1999 movie, *The Sixth Sense*. How long people will recognize the connection is quetionable. There are disturbing aspects to finding this on the tombstone of a sixteen year old boy. One hopes he was only being amusing.

Micah Green (1985-2001)
Gethsemani Catholic Cemetery

Im not left behind
Im on a wing and a prayer

James Tompkins (1955-2005)

Sparlin Cemetery

I'm the boss

> Alice Johnson (1914-1994)
> Mountainside Cemetery

In the line of duty

What duty?

> Elmer Pyle (1886-1938)
> Canyon City Cemetery

It is well with my soul
Come to the garden alone

> Anon
> Lone Fir Cemetery (Portland)

It's the Tibbets bed

> Joe Sheahan (1920-2002)
> Willamette National Cemetery

Let her buck

> W. V. Mattis (1904-1987)
> Fort Rock Cemetery

Let's go from here to become the
wonderful person I created you to be.

Who is speaking here?

> Lisa John (1965-1987)
> Multnomah Park Pioneer Cemetery

Love you past
the rubber
of the universe

> Debra Moore (1963-2011)
> Dayton City Cemetery

Lowroad

> Tommy Highstreet (1950-2007)
> Roseburg National Cemetery

Moroso Motorsports Park

With an engraving of racing motorcyclists.

> Dana Kyle (1960-1992)
> Mountain View Cemetery (Oregon City)

My all & all

> Thomas Moore (1936-2003)
> Willamette National Cemetery

My Dink

> Susan Truluck (1968-1986)
> Silver Lake Cemetery (WA)

Never satisfied—will be back

> Sviatoslav Kudearoff (1930-1992)
> Mount Vernon Cemetery

No diamonds
No Cadillacs

> Robert Neeland (1924-2000)
> Willamette National Cemetery

Ole Missouri

> Marvin Fletcher (1922-2004)
> Alford Cemetery

Pineapple

> Carlos Bazur Jr. (1922-2003)
> Willamette National Cemetery

See you in the morning "Dutchman"
Goodnite

This appears to be a catch-phrase from pop media, but I can't find it. Please advise.

> John (1911-1988) & Anna (b. 1925) Gwyn
> Canyon City Cemetery

Shadrack
Because I can

Shad Tyler
Rock Point/Gold Hill IOOF Cemetery

She was a webel

Ruth "Penny" Arnold (1917-1998)
Mount Pleasant Cemetery

Shortly before his death a white dove sat on the window sill of his father's sleeping room in Pennsylvania

C. G. Wenders (d. 1857)
Rock Creek Cemetery

Skate on Subroza [sic]

Jason Pearce (1983-2001)
Sunset Heights Cemetery

Slimpicker

These single word epitaphs from Willamette National Cemetery have the feel of nick-names. "Nickname" borrowed its initial "n" from the indefinite article, "an." Originally "an ekename" (an "additional name"), it apropriated the "n" to become "a nickname." It makes up for the "n" "naranga" lost to its indefinite article, "a," to become "orange." Karmic orthography.

Michael Hill (1930-1999)
Willamette National Cemetery

Sorry Guys, I had to bounce late.

"Bounce late"? Is there some slang I'm missing?

Benjamin Grant (1983-2005)
Rock Point/Gold Hill IOOF Cemetery

Stay in the buggy

This qualifies as "Advice" if we only knew what it meant.

Kenneth Newton (1935-1995)
Westside Cemetery

The book was finished and was not read

Glenn Morgan (1926-1972)
Mountain View Memorial

The inheriet [sic] laws
matter is the crea-
tor of the universe

Here's a case where I've been unable to extract any comprehension from the epitaph at all. I've tried to guess at the meaning of "inheriet" to no avail; "inherent" is as close as I've come, but even so, it dribbles into confusion. I'll entertain theories.

> William Gilmore (1839-1937)
> Coos River Cemetery

The little boat
That sailed too far from shore

> Matthew Webber (1962-1994)
> Zion Memorial Cemetery (Canby)

The masses seek it,
Few ever find it,
Legend becomes one with it

> Micky (1980-1997)
> Saint Matthew Catholic Cemetery

The only difference in
the sense perception
received from the living,
when compared with the
dead, are those impress-
ions received while in
the presence of the liv-
ing person.
  Lamar

Is this something profound or stating the obvious?

> Lamar Holsheimer (1951-1977)
> Fairview-Scappoose Cemetery

The stitches of her life

> Eloise Cutler (1934-1998)
> Hamilton Cemetery

There is no bush
Too hard to push

Vernon Justen (1948-2003)
Buck Hollow Cemetery

There is no spoon

Apparently, 1999 was a good year for movie quotes. This line is spoken by Spoon Boy in the film, *The Matrix*.

David Merrifield (1951-2003)
Willamette National Cemetery

There once was a
girl from Kelso...

Maxine Niebling (b. 1932)
Forest Lawn Cemetery (Gresham)

There was a wild colonial boy

Is this the beginning of a story or an assessment of character?

Andrew Wynne Sr. (1931-1995)
Fort Klamath Cemetery

They are all par 5s up here

Is this good or bad? I figure, the more chances at making a bad shot that I have, the more bad shots I make.

Kenneth Pillon (1945-1993)
Greenwood Memorial Park

This stone is in tribute to all
living creatures, [sic] that have
suffered and endured man. [sic] In his
quest to control.
John C. Westerfield

John Westerfield (1952-2008)
Mountain View Cemetery (Ashland)

To lend a helping hand

Gladys Montgomery (1917-1999)
Lone Fir Cemetery

Waiting for summer

Drake (1934-2000)
Jacksonville Cemetery

We love you, enjoy your pie.

Richard Kariola (1937-2006)
Bunker Hill Cemetery

Weaver of
Fabrics life [sic]

Fredrick Knapp (1915-2003)
Willamette National Cemetery

Wife of Henry Luce III
Mother of Kenneth D. O'Sullivan
William M. Hurt and James H. Hurt

The truth shall
Make you free

Don't coddle me into the grave. I'm
Going to march into it. I'm a man,
After all.

Not to be confused with Clare Booth Luce, the wife of Henry II. It was Clare, not Claire, who said that LSD gave her a greater appreciation of colors. Yes, it will do that. I have corresponded with Mr. Hurt, the actor, on the provenance of his mother's epitaph, but he hasn't gotten back to me, as yet. She must have been quite some guy.

Claire Luce (1923-1971)
Fort Harney Cemetery

Why seek the living here

Violet Olson (1915-2005)
Skyline Memorial Cemetery

You never know[,] boys...

A case of a lost comma highlighting an important distinction.

Richard Roskopf (1936-1994)
Finley-Sunset Hills Cemetery

FRIENDS, ROMANS, COUNTRYMEN
(EULOGIES)

For the most part, eulogies are written by the survivors, though ocassionally someone likes to toot their own horn. They are arranged by death date, where known, otherwise a birth date, if available; within a given year, they're arranged alphabetically by first line. Those without are gathered at the end of the chapter in alphabetical order of first lines. Reading them, especially the early ones, provides a sometimes harrowing, often amazing, glimpse into the days of white settlement. It's hard to always remember that, from the native perspective, the arrival of the settlers was the equivalent of Atilla and the Huns showing up for diner; and that perspective is rarely shown in epitaphs. Reading them offers a fascinating, if select, window onto the history of the territory. Military service shows up beyond its proportion.

Some epitaphs honor their subject; others are more perfunctory: "Just the facts, ma'am." Some hone in on one facet of a person's life; others provide a broad sweep of assessment. Some are poetic and some are worthy of a middling clerk. Some are humble, some are exalted. Whichever they are, they shine a light on who lies buried there. A little bit of them breaks off and comes home with us.

Beneath this sod
The first ever broken in Oregon
For the reception of a
White mother and child
Lies the remains of
Anna Maria Pittman
First wife of
Rev. Jason Lee
And their infant son
She sailed from New York in July 1836
Landed in Oregon June 1837
Was married July 15, 1837
And died
June 26, 1838

> Anna Pittman (1803-1838)
> Lee Mission Cemetery

Sacred
to the memory of
M. John Charles, Jun.(r)
who unfortunately lost his life by
the accidental discharge of a gun
in the hands of his companion

and fellow traveller
on the 21 of October 1849
in the 22nd year of his age.
Much and deservedly regretted
by his friends and conne[c]tions

> John Charles Jr. (1827-1849)
> Vancouver Barracks Post Cemetery

Worked with the early settlers and requested they be bur-
ied in the white man's cemetery

> Indian Clark (d. 1850) & Indian Jim (d. 1850)
> Yamhill-Carlton Cemetery

Drowned in Snake River west of Boise, Idaho, en
route to Oregon with his family and his brothers' families

> Obediah Hines (1805-1853)
> Lee Mission Cemetery

Born in Quebec
Died at Oregon City
Fur trader and explorer
in Old Oregon
Arrived Columbia River 1818
Clerk of North West Company
Chief Factor Hudson's Bay
Company at Fort Vancouver
Rescued Survivors of
Whitman massacre 1847

Peter was a larger-than-life figure who cut a broad swath through the West; Ogden, Utah, is named after him. His journals are available online and are illuminating reading.

> Peter Skene Ogden (1794-1854)
> Mountain View Cemetery (Oregon City)

Joel Coffey was born June 15, 1789, in Wilkesboro, TN, the
son of Chesley Coffey and Margaret Baldwyn. His wife,
Sarah Mackey, died in 1851 in Boonesville, MO. He took
his children, Amanda, Elizabeth Angeline, Alexander L.,
Terrel Mackey, and Mary Louisa across the Oregon Trail
arriving in Clark County, WA, in 1852. Coffey received
a 160-acre land grant in Fern Prairie. Shortly before his

death his daughter married into the Van Vleet family. He
was laid to rest in what is now known as Fern Prairie
Cemetery.

Joel Coffey (1789-1855)
Fern Prairie Cemetery

First circuit rider in this area
Emigrated to Oregon from Missouri in 1846
on the first wagon train up the treacherous
Southern Oregon route. Took a land claim on
the Santiam. Organized the first churches of any
faith in the valley. "Elder Joe," preacher, singer,
farmer, father, faithfully rode circuit through
rain, sickness and danger.
　　To honor his memory this memorial
is erected by the Turnidge Clan
　　1973

Joseph Turnidge (1819-1857)
Miller Cemetery (Millersburg)

Killed in battle with the Snake
Indians xxx Crooked River, Ogn.
May 13, 1864

Steven Watson (Lieut.) (1828-1864)
Vancouver Barracks Post Cemetery

Nahum King (1783-1856) and Sarepta Norton King (1791-
　　1864) married in 1807 in
Columbia County, New York where Sarepta was born.
　　Nahum's family migrated
there from New Salem, Massachusetts, his birthplace.
　　Daughters Saretta and
Lucretia were born in New York. Fourteen more King chil-
　　dren were born in
Madison County, Ohio, where the family settled in about
　　1810. Thirty years later
the family moved to Carroll County, Missouri.

In 1845, Nahum and Sarepta, with twenty-four family
　　members, headed west to
Oregon. Persuaded to take a shortcut across eastern Or-

135

egon, they suffered terrible
hardships on the Meek Cutoff, including the death of
   Sarah King Chambers near the
Malheur River. Far behind other wagons, exhausted and
   starving, they reached The
Dalles and the daunting Columbia. Rafting the Columbia,
   John Susan King and
two children were lost. The Kings wintered in Portland. In
   early 1846 hunting
for land, they found this beautiful green valley and staked
   their claims here. Nahum
and Sarepta rest in an unmarked grave on their family
   claim near Wren. Many other
Kings lived out their lives here in what is today Kings
   Valley.

> Nahum (1783-1856) & Sarepta (1791-1864) King
> Kings Valley Cemetery

Veteran of War of 1812
Son of veteran of American Revolution
Oregon pioneer 1843

> John Holman (1787-1861)
> Masonic Cemetery (McMinnville)

A pioneer:
The first settler in Lane Co. 1846

A man's life is his monument
His deeds are the inscription

> E[lijah] Bristow (1788-1872)
> Pleasant Hill Cemetery (Pleasant Hill)

Captain of first wagon train
to cross
Rocky Mountains 1843

> David Lenox (1807-1873)
> West Union Baptist Cemetery

Rev. W. A. Verboort
Born in Holland
Oct. 23, 1835

136

Emigrated to Wis. U. S. A.
in 1848 Commenced his
studies in 1857 was
ordained priest in 1863
Came to Ore. in 1875
Died July 14, 1876
Aged 40 yrs.

> W. A. Verboort (1835-1876)
> Visitation Cemetery

A pioneer of the 40s
Sometimes called
Father of Oregon Waters

> Leonard White (1835-1878)
> Lone Fir Cemetery (Portland)

Born in Baltimore MD.
Killed by Indians in
Grant Co. Or. during the
Raid of the Bannock
and Piute tribes
in June 1878
Age 23 years

> James Daulby (1855-1878)
> Canyon City Cemetery

Pioneer of 1842 - just 1 year old, she was the youngest
*   child*
To cross the Plains from Missouri in the wagon train of
*   1842.*

> Mary Shadden-Hembree (1841-1880)
> Masonic Cemetery (McMinnville)

His life was beautiful
His death triumphant
His work abiding

> Anon (1820-1881)
> Lee Mission Cemetery

Pioneer of 1850 - her mother, Martha Eliza Shadden, was
*   pregnant*

137

When she rode the "Trapper's Trail" from Oregon to
Sutter's Fort
In 1843. Eliza Jane, born August 30, 1843, was the first
child born
In California to an emigrant family that had crossed the
plains

Eliza Shadden-Wallan (1843-1883)
Masonic Cemetery (McMinnville)

Missionary to native tribes, 1839
First white woman in
Tualatin settlement, July, 1841.
First white mother in same, Nov. 8, 1842
Continued as helping missionary
Till death, Sept. 22, 1884, in her 80th yr.

Desire Griffin (1806-1884)
Masonic Cemetery (Hillsboro)

Who brought the Covenant
for this, the first Baptist church
west of the Rocky mountains.

William Beagle (1808-1887)
West Union Baptist Cemetery

The first white settler, the first county clerk, and taught
the first school in Tillamool County.

Joseph C. Champion lived at Kechis Point, on Tillamook
Bay, April 1, 1851, having come from Astoria in a whale
boat with two companions, who returned with the boat
the next day. He lived in a hollow spruce tree, which he
called his castle[,] for the first three months.

Joseph Champion (1823-1891)
Tillamook IOOF Cemetery

Born in Breslau, Germany about 1850. Died by
drowning October 22, 1892 in Linnton, Oregon.
His wife Seana Elizabeth Peters who was Seana Birt
of Woodland, Washington died September 15, 1900
in British Columbia leaving 2 children
Hazel & Otto Peters and 2 grandchildren

138

Charles Edward Barks and Robert Woodrow Barks.
Written by his mother. Dec. 23, 1936

Otto Peters (d. 1892)
Masonic Cemetery (St. Helens)

Drowned

There is rest in
Heaven. His record
is on high.

Ollie Williams (1872-1894)
Cedar Hill Cemetery (Oakland)

Pioneer of 1842. Signer of the "Wolves Letter."
Took his family to California with Lansford Hastings in
1843.
Made his fortune during the gold rush of 1849.
Brought his family back to Oregon in 1850.
This cemetery is part of his original farm.
His built his home of Baker Creek Road in 1859.
It is still standing after nearly 150 years.

Thomas Shadden (1809-1894)
Masonic Cemetery (McMinnville)

The daughter of Chief Sealth for
whom the city of Seattle is named
was a life long supporter of the
white settlers. She was converted
to Christianity and named by
Mrs. D. S. Maynard.

Princess Angeline befriended the
pioneers during the Indian attack
upon Seattle on January 26, 1856.
At her request she was laid to
rest near her protector and friend,
Henry L. Yesler.
    Seattle Historical Society
        1958

Princess Angeline (1811-1896)
Lake View Cemetery (Seattle)

Was a pioneer of 1846, served in the
Cayuse Indian War, and was one of the
party who rescued the women and chil-
dren who were taken prisoners by
the Indians at the Whitman Massacre, which
took place in the fall of 1847.

James Leabo (1823-1898)
Multnomah Park Cemetery

D. C. A.
Venville
Born
Jan. 8, 1881
Who was wounded
and captured with
Lieut. Gilmore
of the U. S. Navy, on
April 12, 1899
at Baler, Luzon, P. I.
and was treacher-
ously murdered
by order of Novicio,
an Insurgent Genl.
some time after
Feb. 20, 1890.

We know not where
his body lies,
but his spirit is
with God.

D. C. A. Venville (1881-1900)
Milwaukie Pioneer Cemetery

Born DeKalb Co., Mo.
Arrived at Cascades by ox team in 1852
Married Margaret Windsor 1853
1854 built & owned steamer "Wasco"
1855 donation land claim of 323 acres
1858 worked on upper Cascades block house
Built & owned 2 sawmills
Built 1st school. For short time saloon owner.

Felix Iman (1828-1902)
Iman Cemetery

In
Memory of
Samuel and Huldah
Colver
Pioneers of 1850 who located
this Donation Claim in 1851
amid hostile Indians
and who have seen
the wilderness
blossom
as the
rose

Samuel & Huldah (1823-1907) Colver
Phoenix Pioneer Cemetery

A soldier in the Seminole War of 1837
The Mexican War of 1846
An Indian War veteran
Cayuse War 1855
also
A volunteer fireman
City of Portland, Oregon
A friend to all

John Parkhill (1816-1910)
Lone Fir Cemetery (Portland)

He was pleasant to live with.

Is this damning with faint praise?

Walter Ross (1871-1910)
Lyle-Balch Cemetery

She hath done
What she could

Nora Whitman (1862-1910)
Tutuilla Presbyterian Indian Mission Cemetery

Erected by his friends to the memory of

141

Oregon's world-renowned Cartoonist

Homer Davenport (1867-1912)
Silverton Cemetery

Veteran of Battle
of Nashville Tenn
under Col. Grigsby

John Smith (1839-1912)
Cove Cemetery

Last survivor of the 52 persons that formed the first civil
government west of the Rockies on May 2, 1843

F. X. Matthieu (1819-1914)
Butteville Cemetery

Pvt. Henry H. Bruce
son of
J. F. and Nora Bruce
Entered U.S. service
June 24, 1918
Assigned to Co. B. 77th Div.
308th Inf. in France
Killed in action, Argonne Forest
Sept. 26, 1918
Aged 28 years, 8 months

Henry Bruce (1890-1918)
Enterprise Cemetery

Mr. Klinger built the first ice plant
in the City of Salem in June 1888. Also
the first lager beer brewery Aug. 1, 1877.

Maurice Klinger (1844-1919)
Saint Barbaras Cemetery

In memory of
Indian "Lize"
Last of the Calapooyas
Died in 1921
Age about 100 years
Buried in this pioneer cemetery
Linn Co. Pioneer Memorial Assoc.

142

Indian Lize (d. 1921)
Brownsville Pioneer Cemetery

The legendary Cabin Lake fly
fisherman and fishing consultant,
specializing in bizarre theories in
fly fishing

4 Wood Hull Ave.
Bayside, Long Island
New York

Aside from being a rare example of a eulogy being written by the pre-deceased, this is the only case I've encountered of someone putting their address on their tombstone. What happens if he ends up in an old people's home before he dies? Not to mention, is he a legend in his own mind? We can only imagine the fishing theories.

William Barchuck (b. 1921)
Fort Rock Cemetery

World War II B-17 Inspector

Grace Byrnes (b. 1921)
Cove Cemetery

From 1942 to 1945 he was in the U. S. Armed Guard and
sailed on Liberty Ships and a T. 2. oil tanker. 1946 to 1965
he worked on tug boats. 1965 he joined the Columbia
River Pilots Association. He piloted about 4000 cargo ves-
sels from Astoria to Portland. The largest supertanker he
piloted was:

Under which, running the length of the stone, is an engraving of the "S. S. American Spirit/ 1102 feet long by 178 feet wide."

Gunners mate 3rd class M. H. Ringering was a 5 inch 38
caliber anti air craft specialist. In charge of a eleven man
crew. In the Armed Guard he sailed to New Caledonia, Es-
piritu Santos, Samoa, Eniwetok, Solomon Island. Guada-
canal, Saipan and Honolulu. On board a C2 cargo vessel
anchored in Okinawa harbor near the city of Naha in the
spring of 1945 he and his crew stayed in their gun tub 22
days and nights shooting down Japanese suicide planes
coming in at all hours. 6 ships were sunk in the harbor, but

his load of bombs, heavy equipment and barrels of gaso-
line were saved. His last voyage was aboard a T2 tanker
with a cargo of B52 aircraft fuel sailing to the island of
Tinian where the atomic bomb took off from.

Merlin Ringering (b. 1922)
Robert Bird Cemetery

His life was gentle.
His spirit kind.
To all mankind most benign.

Jacob Fake (1828-1923)
Sparta Cemetery

Born at Tippecanoe Co., Ind.
1852 Missouri to The Dalles on horse back
Carried motherless babe 500 miles
Took raft downriver to Cascades
1853 met and married Felix G. Iman
Survived Indian War of Mar. 26, 1856
Indians burned home
Had 16 children, 9 boys, 7 girls

Margaret was not born in DeKalb Co. Her mother died when she was young, and after moving to DeKalb, Margaret eventually ran away from home to escape an abusive step-mother and joined a wagon-train heading for Oregon. She never spoke of her early life. It was Margaret who made me realize we had Founding Mothers more than Founding Fathers.

Margaret Iman (1834-1924)
Iman Cemetery

Judge of Lake County 1912-1924
Founder of Lake County roads

At his request his friends rolled this stone
from off the hills he loved — to mark his final resting
place

E. H. Smith (1873-1924)
IOOF Cemetery (Lakeview)

Veteran WWII, adventurer, explorer, navigator, pilot
40 years pioneering airfreight with the Flying Tiger Line.
Received "Gold Air Medal" in 1971 as world's outstand-

144

ing sport
Pilot. Institute of Navigation award for "superior achievement,"
Air Line Pilots' award for "outstanding airmanship." Holder of
Fifteen world records and firsts. First man to circle the earth
Solo via the poles. First man to cross Antarctica alone. Author of
Books on Amelia Earhart, and the Oregon Wagon Train of 1842.

Elgen Long (b. 1927)
Masonic Cemetery (McMinnville)

A war bride and war worker, who by
personal experience knew of the grim
toll demanded by war and yet never
swerved from doing her full duty. In
peace time "personally" and through the
Amer. Leg. Aux., she did much to make
easier the lot of the veteran and his family.

Nellie Husted (1881-1929)
Jefferson Cemetery

Lt. Col. U.S. Army
Korean War 1952-53
Berlin Wall 1961-62

Edward Geer (b. 1929)
Sacred Heart Cemetery (Lake Oswego)

First Japanese woman settler in Oregon

Miyo Iwakoshi (1852-1931)
White Birch Cemetery

Drowned in the aid of a
stricken craft Feb. 26, 1935

George Meadows (1910-1935)
Pacific Sunset Cemetery

Frank David McCully
the Father of Wallowa County

145

was buried in this Indian cemetery because of long
friendship with Chief Joseph and his people.

Frank McCully (1859-1939)
Old Chief Joseph Grave Site

A life of charity, forgiveness, and kindness
to others — her song, in a sweet pleasant voice,
came from her heart; and she loved not only
in word and tongue, but in deed and truth.

Maisie Caldwell (1885-1940)
Buxton Cemetery

Father of the cheese industry in the Oregon Country

Peter McIntosh (1861-1940)
Hills Cemetery

Died concentration camp

Moses Weiss (d. 1943)
Ahavai Shalom Cemetery

In memory of
Alvin Johnson
1878 • 1947
By his friends and
fellow employees of the
White Pine Lumber Co.

Alvin Johnson (1878-1947)
Sunset Park Cemetery

Nursed as a profession
Trusted and upright

J. E. Ehrlich (1877-1947)
Municipal/Lakeview Cemeteries

To serve his state and his people
was to Frank Irvine a beautiful
adventure, a privilege without
price, a responsibility without
limitations, a liberty too precious
to be appraised. In humble words

and simple sentences he capitalized
the human side of journalism.
He was a great American

> B. F. Irvine (1868-1954)
> Rose City Cemetery

Proprietor of Grants
Pass last livery stable

> Guy Gravlin (1886-1955)
> Pioneer Masonic Cemetery (Grants Pass)

Postmaster, barber, wheat rancher, merchant

> Harry Long (1888-1957)
> Masonic Cemetery (McMinnville)

First white boy born in Wallowa Valley

> Lorn Powers (1874-1964)
> Bramlet Memorial Cemetery

King of the Gypsies

This was neither metaphorical, allegorical, nor wishful thinking, merely a job description.

> Frank Ellis (1905-1966)
> Rose City Cemetery

Lost his life in an airplane crash near Arctic Village,
Alaska, on April 3, 1971.

> Dan Johnson (1946-1971)
> Roseburg Cemetery

Great beauty of person
"The gift of winning speech
A mind that mastered readily
Whatever it cared to master.
Poetry and the love of all
Beautiful things.
A heart as tender as it was brave.
Only one gift was
Withheld from her,
Length of years."

Barbara A. (1932-1973)
Lebanon Odd Fellows and Masonic Cemetery

*A mass spectrometer engineer who was
the best at what he did.... An inquiring
mind, patient, a perfectionist, a teacher
— he cared. He has a free spirit, which
allowed him to march though life by
his own drum beat.... We should remember that life is for the living. John
would be the first to say, "Make the
best of it."*
   John Cornelius

John Ramsay (1940-1974)
Logtown Cemetery

*Born at Yainax Indian Agency, grandson of Old
Sheepie. A respected member of the Klamath Tribe
and dedicated 45 years working in Klamath tribal
affairs.*

Boyd Jackson Sr. (1888-1974)
Chief Schonchin Cemetery

*Our beloved son and brother
who raced through life
now rests in peace*

It's hard to appreciate from afar the impact Steve had on Oregon and Eugene in particular. People still leave memorials at his crash site. He was so much more than a
world-class runner, although it would be hard to credit anything more than the zeit-
geist of the times. Sunset Memorial is a lawn cemetery, but they make an exception for
Mr. Prefontaine; he's as great a star as Coos Bay is likely to have.

Steve Prefontaine (1951-1975)
Sunset Memorial Park (Coos Bay)

*31st Infantry
Bataan survivor*

Denton Rees (1907-1977)
Willamette National Cemetery

"Grandma Tootsie"

148

A woman of warmth and love; a woman of caring and kindness; a person who always put someone else before/ herself. Should we mourn her leaving us?... Her thoughtfulness on each of our/ special occasions. Her great sense of humor. Her hospitality and warmth to all visitors. Her delicious/ Christmas meals, and, of course, Santa Claus, Always the surprises at Easter, and there was the family/ Thanksgiving with her homemade pumpkin pies and hot rolls. No other person could have set a better/ example than you. Grandma, we will miss you, but we'll never! never! forget, and we'll always be proud.
    Your Grandchildren

            Leona Courtney (1901-1978)
            Sunset Cemetery (Ontario)

She brought her songs, dances, and kindness to America to brighten our lives.

            Lizzie Ireland (1897-1978)
            Gales Creek Cemetery

A surgeon who spent his life mending people

            H. Minor Nichols (1908-1979)
            Frank Abel Cemetery

He was like a tea rose A little rough with a few thorns But through the thorns you could Always see the rose

He gave his life   Everything And asked for nothing He was a man and true father

            Loren Mackey (1913-1979)
            Cascade Locks Cemetery

Soldier's solace, doctor's wife, gifted organizer Partner in adventure, lover and mother

Both descendants of John Alder and Priscilla

Three centuries later by diverse paths
Linked again our families
Here in Oregon

On this further westward trek
In this peacefulness at Pike
Here waits my darling Kae
Among these pioneers

> Katherine Perkin (1920-1979)
> Pike-North Yamhill Cemetery

Born in Arnsfeld, Prussia Apr. 10, 1924,
she endured mistreatment from Russians
at the end of World War II from which
she suffered the rest of her life and
died July 22, 1980.

> Waltraut Ericsson (1924-1980)
> Pleasant Hill Cemetery (Pleasant Hill)

Royal Canadian
Mounted Police
Corporal
Northern Patrol

> Clint Crombie (1895-1981)
> Bunker Hill Cemetery

Bambi Lynn Marshall
Born 1962 Zama, Japan
Married 1980 Tahoe, Nevada
Died 1982
Marshall Ranch, Wamic, Oregon.

> Bambi Marshall (1962-1982)
> Saint Mary's Cemetery (Hood River)

He suffered   He gave
He asked for nothing
Let him rest in eternal love

> Sid Myron (1909-1982)
> United Church of Christ Cemetery (Ten O'Clock
> Church)

A lover of all wild things and a friend of the wilderness.
Hunter, fisherman, outdoorsman. A Boy Scout and active
in all sports.
Paul was always at his family's side and his friends were
many.
He had a world of love and the good times we had will
never be forgotten through the canyons, mountains and
deserts he loved so much.
Kind to the little guy and underdog and loved by the older
people and cared,
We layed [sic] him to rest in view of his beloved hunting
grounds in Radersburg, Montana.

Paul Barnett (1965-1983)
IOOF Cemetery (Grass Valley)

Member Polish Underground Home Army
Warsaw Uprising 1943
Honor: Bronze Cross of Merit with Swords
World War II 1939-1944
Beloved
Sister, Wife, Mother, Grandmother

Eugenia Rett-Wilczkowiak (1921-1983)
Danish Cemetery

Mother was strength. Little
did we know how strong till
understanding came with age.

Minnie Chord (1894-1983)
Pleasant Hill Cemetery (Pleasant Hill)

Doug,
like the wind — high-spirited,
yet gentle and elusive.
Impossible
to catch or to hold;
Full of adventure, wonder,
and nonsense.
How do we let him go?

Douglas Aller (1959-1984)
Grandview Cemetery

151

She dances in our hearts.

> Judy Woods (1949-1985)
> Bonney Cemetery

Linda was the most unorganized-organized person I've ever met. She was 41 going on 18, a precious little girl, yet a grown mature woman, Linda was stubborn yet giving; weak yet strong; simple yet complex.

Linda had a never ending supply of energy which she shared with all who knew her. She was always honest and open. When she said she cared, you knew she really did.

Linda was 4'11" - 10' tall. I can still hear that tell tale snap of her gum. Linda was always an all or nothing person, and even though it seems we're left with nothing, we really have her all.

> Linda Clark (1945-1986)
> Valley View Cemetery

Worlds [sic] first smokejumper
to parachute to a fire
Nez Perce National Forest
July 12, 1940

> Rufus Robinson (1905-1987)
> Wallowa Cemetery

A strong and gentle man who walked
To the beat of his own drummer

> Frederick Pugh (1931-1988)
> Greencrest Memorial Park

An American cowboy

> Roy Gatliff (1918-1988)
> Bonney Cemetery

She gave so much and demanded so little

> Eileen Novak (1945-1988)
> Pratum Cemetery

From wagon wheels to space ships

> Lillace (b. 1907) & Lawrence (1902-1989) Walton

Estacada IOOF Cemetery

Leaving 98 descendants
To mourn her

> Grace Walker (1900-1989)
> Multnomah Park Pioneer Cemetery

The old buck

> Robert Boedigheimer (1929-1989)
> Saint Mary Catholic Cemetery

She who taught us about birds and flowers soars forever
brightly in our hearts.

> M. Ruth Schmerber (1934-1990)
> Saint Louis Cemetery

The eternal optimist

> Adolf Tischler (1902-1990)
> Havurah Shalom Cemetery

A deeply devoted and loving Husband, Father, Grandfather, Great Grandfather and Friend, he tackled life with unrivaled passion. Self-educated, strong willed, patriotic, proud, fearless and fun-loving, he was a pioneer in his industry and a community leader. Abiding his own counsel, he sought to be judged by the strength of his principles: honesty, loyalty, fairness, perseverance, temperance and respect for others.

"Gramps" wrote the following words in one of his many
letters to his grandchildren:

"As you reach for the sky you must realize that there may
be may pitfalls on the way but anything worth having
is worth struggling for."

His magical spirit lives on and will inspire us forever

> Max Lesman (1908-1991)
> Ahavai Shalom Cemetery

To Our Mother

*You are now free to soar with
the sea gulls, watch the majestic
waves break, or walk along the
tranquil beach as you did when
you were young. You did not do
great things, just small things
with great love. Our love for you
will be in our hearts for eternity.*

Lauri (1913-1982) & Phyllis Maki (1924-1991)
Hudson Cemetery

*A friendly smile
A caring heart
A generous spirit
Was a natural art
A strong faith in God
A love of life
A healthy mix of all
    This, my wife*

Ellen Phillips (1917-1992)
Island City Cemetery

A sports fan and "mensch"

Harry Pearlman (1918-1992)
Neveh Zedek Cemetery

*With love and patience,
  they raised three Sons.
With intelligence,
  they taught them how to survive and prosper.
With wisdom,
  they let them discover the world for themselves.*

Mathew (1917-1987) & Lillian (1921-1992) Black
Dallas Cemetery

*A good farmer, a loving son, a friend to us all
But as a husband you just stood out from the rest*

Robert Smutz (1939-1993)
Grandview Cemetery

154

The Mad Russian of Oysterville

> Norman Dutchuk (1929-1993)
> Oysterville Cemetery

Together they built Quailhurst

> Ben (1924-1993) & Lynden (1941-1986) Langston
> Pleasant View Cemetery

Colonel U.S.A.F.
A retired fighter pilot who served in Vietnam
His ashes are scattered over his
Favorite hunting area in Central Oregon

> Robert Hanna (1931-1994)
> Odd Fellows Cemetery (Myrtle Creek)

He lived life laughing, and left life living.

> Larry Rogers (1974-1994)
> Lone Fir Cemetery (Portland)

He was neither the Sunrise, nor the Sunset. He was the Sun.

> Brian O'Grady (1960-1994)
> Ocean View Cemetery

Her spirit soared to the boundless heights
Into a celestial canopy forever bright
Reflecting love and faith and a life ever giving
Her legacy a blessing to whoever shared her

> Shirley Tanzer (1929-1994)
> Ahavai Shalom Cemetery

Native American
An individualist
With eternal spirit

> Dale Smith (1930-1994)
> Mountain View Cemetery (Oregon City)

Pioneered the introduction
of pastrami into the
United States and Jewish culture

155

Benjamin Deutsch (1912-1994)
Havurah Shalom Cemetery

Strength to survive war
Courage to seek new shores

Pleun (1911-1989) & Elizabeth (1912-1994) Visser
Lone Fir Cemetery (Portland)

The first psychoanalyst of Clark County
Art is long, life is short

B. Russell Eby (1951-1994)
Sara Union Cemetery

The most loving young man
We've known
Died profoundly awash in love
And lives today the same

Aaron Dunsmore (1974-1994)
Saint Edward Cemetery

The power and majesty of an unbridled spirit

Holly Sickles (1977-1994)
Unknown cemetery in Montana or Idaho

CIA scout for Free Laos
American citizen

Txhia Cha (1955-1995)
Gethsemani Catholic Cemetery

Killed with his two companions by an
avalanche after making the first successful
ascent of Mr. Orville, Fair Weather Range, Alaska.

Patrick Simmons (1957-1995)
Northwood Park Cemetery

The people's politician and his loving wife.
During his tenure on the City Council
(1967-1991), Seattle became America's
most livable city.

Samuel (1922-1995) & Marion (1925-1991) Smith
Mount Pleasant Cemetery (Seattle)

Chetnik & freedom fighter

Chetniks, according to *Wikipedia*, "were a Serbian nationalist and royalist paramilitary organization operating in the Balkans before and during the World Wars, mostly known for their participation in the Yugoslav Front of World War II."

Voiin Janicic (1915-1996)
Aumsville Cemetery

The best kid on the block

Brian Ownesby (1972-1996)
Bethany Pioneer Cemetery (Silverton)

What was lacking in education
Was overflowing with knowledge.

Earl "Pat" Wyscaver (1930-1996)
Claggett Cemetery

Born Edward L. Hart
in Oregon March 18, 1905
Came to Twin Rocks in 1912
Enjoyed the lumber Merchant
Marine and cheese industries
And everything God made
Died Wheeler Oct. 18, 1997

Ed Hart (1905-1997)
American Legion Cemetery

Descendant of
1st settler of Oregon Territory
Etienne Lussie & Felicite Niute

Mary Roemaine (1912-1997)
Old Carson Cemetery

In the sea of life some people make ripples,
Trisha
Made waves

Trisha Nodurft (1982-1998)
Mountain View Cemetery (Oregon City)

157

No man is indispensable,
but some are irreplaceable

> Charles (1941-1998)
> Fern Hill Cemetery (Menlo)

Exceeds beyond mediocrity
Very outgoing, charming and funny
Has a smooth way of talking
His feelings get hurt easily
God upholds him and keeps him true
Tries to be a man of his word
Always moving - never at rest
He learns fast - quick to action
To remain adventurous and daring

Pray to God, Ronald's family never sees this; but this epitaph has haunted me for years. The cemetery overlooks the Federal Penitentiary in Sheridan, OR and this epitaph has always felt like a mother's notes to be presented in front of a parole board. The combination of "exceeds beyond mediocrity" and "tries go be a man of his word" are grudging words of praise. There are too many lines to read between. They are painful. Perhaps I project.

> Ronald Smith (1957-1999)
> Greencrest Memorial Park

He defended his country
In WWII and helped build
His country in peace

> Norman McMurrin (1922-1999)
> Jefferson Cemetery

Through life these hands built so much
for others, for his family he built
"A Home of Love"

> Billy Powell (1931-1999)
> Adams Cemetery

Wonderful Wife, Mom & Maggo

Smiled when near
Made the rain disappear
Life abundant full and free

We all love & miss you forever

Charlotte Baker (1946-1999)
Logan-Pleasant ViewCemetery

Writer. Wordsmith.
Chronicler of Oysterville

Well-remembered, do you lie
on the hill in graveyard square

It would do you well to visit Oysterville, WA during the November gales to get a full appreciation of where Willard worked. Look it up on a map, if you will. Take one of his books with you and visit its fairyland cemetery. *Wikipedia* says, "Willard Richardson Espy was a U.S. editor, philologist, writer, and poet. He is particularly remembered for his anthology of light verse and word play, *An Almanac of Words at Play*, and its two sequels. His writing and poetry regularly appeared in *Punch, Reader's Digest,* and *Word Ways.*" He made us folks on the coast look a lot smarter than we are.

Willard (1910-1999) & Louise (b. 1919) Espy
Oysterville Cemetery

Alma, dau. of Lester Daniels & Gertrude Rice. Worked
hard beside her husband as logging camp cook, bar
maid & mother. Artistic. She sewed, knitted, crocheted,
painted & wrote.

Alma always got her deer

Alma Whitlow (1918-2000)
Pike-North Yamhill Cemetery

B. 1911 Lewiston, MT, (photo) 1928 Fergus High grad
(honors, marching band), California nurse 1929-32, m. at
Seattle 1935, four babies: Vail, Bob, Pat, Mike 1937-43,
single working mom 1948-63, business graduate Univer-
sity of Washington 1967, retired 1984. Laid here to rest in
forever loving memory by her children. She was tall, slim,
pretty, thrifty, compassionate, hard-working. She gave
every effort her very best; loved her family, Montana, real
estate, children, music, good books, Shakespeare, seafood,
big trees, car camping, her home of 52 years, her angel. Our
thanks to:

Designer: William Cantelon/Quiring Monuments

Sculpture: Karen Stocker/bronze casting: Robert Morten-
son/amateur-contest winning photo: Walter Lehman/
foundation: Pat Kelly/plaque: A. M. S. 2002.

Catherine Kelly (1911-2000)
Greenwood Cemetery (Cathlamet)

Bigger than life, he leaves us with
a most colorful palette of memories

Albert Ieronemo (1945-2000)
Saint Mary's Cemetery (Corvallis)

He left a
Trail of truth

Don (1909-1984) & Ruby (1913-2000) McFarling
Oswego Pioneer Cemetery

He left his family in Cuba,
Though they always remained in his heart.
His friends he made part of his family here
As he knew he must make a new start.

And he showed us such love,
And so many loved him
That though he's not with us,
We're still not apart.

Reyaldo Penton (1960-2000)
Mount Calvary Catholic Cemetery

Here lies a young man who at the age of 20
had earned the respect of his elders and his
competitors and was a true friend to all.
An ackomplishment [sic] made by few at any age.
We are proud to have had the honor of
calling him son and brother.
Thank you Donnie, you made a difference.

Donnie Heaton III (1980-2000)
Merrill IOOF Cemetery

Loving husband father
Creative tinkerer

Higdon (1912-2000)
Willamette National Cemetery

A quiet man with a lot to say

Floyd Taylor (1911-2001)
Pine Haven Cemetery

Beloved father, mother, & grandparents
United in working for peace & justice

Sol (1925-1990) & Geraldine (1929-2001) Peck
Havurah Shalom Cemetery

A smile for every stranger

Marjorie Lee (1916-2002)
Pilot Butte-Greenwood Cemetery

He simply
Enjoyed life

Lawrence Wong (1919-2002)
Willamette National Cemetery

He was known
As Bud

Virgil Tibbetts (1927-2002)
Willamette National Cemetery

Incredible mind, charming, witty, intelligent,
lover of nature, kind, generous, only brother,
poet, appreciator of higher thought, person
of ideas, a gentle man and a gentleman,
chef extraordinaire, only son, proud uncle,
no finer more loyal friend, lover of the ocean,
protector of those he loved, grower, maker
and appreciator of the finer things in life.
   Tom, we miss you

Thomas Archibald (1960-2002)
River View Cemetery

One good man

William Nelson (1923-2002)

Oregon's Man of the Past

William "Smokey" Humbird (1920-2002)
Damascus Cemetery

Our ol' Sea Daddy

Thomas McInturff (1924-2002)
Willamette National Cemetery

Story teller

Ralph Prouty (1927-2002)
Willamette National Cemetery

The lady that liked kids
Always on the sunnyside

Jean Widenoja (1941-2002)
Fort Rock Cemetery

A pair to
Draw to

Frank & Constance (1924-2003) Schnoor
Willamette National Cemetery

National Honor Society student, mother of 2, executive assistant
Publicist, author, mentor, founder of an aerospace museum
A remarkable and caring woman who could get things done

Marie Kurilich-Long (1925-2003)
Masonic Cemetery (McMinnville)

This farmer sowed generosity

Gordon Larson (1913-2003)
Sara Union Cemetery

Served in the
Special Guerilla Units (SGU)
Royal Armed Forces (FAR)
in Laos from 1960 to 1975

in the Vietnam War

Xiong Pao Lee (1930-2003)
Columbia Memorial Cemetery

A straight shooter that
worked through adversity

Richard Widenoja (1944-2004)
Fort Rock Cemetery

Angels danced the
day she was born

Grace Tower (1916-2004)
River View Cemetery

Started many AA meetings
Saved many lives

Jerry Bogle (1936-2004)
Kinder Cemetery

Strong, Brave, Diligent is your nature
Optimism and Love lead to your Successes
Suffering and unfairness have forever gone
Eternity is for you to enjoy the forever peace...

You came to the world with a great promise
To bring up a super family like planting a huge tree
Started with nothing but an excellent seed
Carries a pair of heavy baskets for its nursery
Stretched its roots deep throughout the Earth
Stood guarding it in the raging storms...

All your efforts have become fruitful;
Twelve children and ten branching families
Numerous grandchildren and their offspring
Will forever appreciate your responsibilities
Forever memorize your honor and your glories...

Dong Zhi Chen (1915-2004)
Lincoln Memorial Cemetery

The Cowboy
Preacher

163

Who rode into Glory
With his boots on!

Hand-carved onto wooden headboard.

> Rodger Hall (1938-2004)
> Camp Polk Cemetery

With music in his soul

> Harry York (1910-2004)
> Neveh Zedek Cemetery

A man at home in nature.

> Michael Simmons (1957-2005)
> Northwood Park Cemetery

An old buzzard lives here

> Richard Shepard (1931-2005)
> Saint Patrick's Historic Cemetery

Cowboy pastor
Loved by
God & family

> Lyle Jeffers (1930-2005)
> Fort Rock Cemetery

Dear Ray,
    You will be remembered for the rainbow you were in our rainy days, for the gentleness, kindness and compassion you always offered your family, friends and even strangers, for the ability to put others first, and for your greatest passions - your students, your cats and your love of music. We will always love and miss you but most of all we will remember you for the shining star you were and forever will be.
    We love you,
    Your Family and Friends

> Raymundo Becerra (1975-2005)
> Rest Lawn Memorial Park

Fisherman skydiver cook
71 and 420 friendly

"420 friendly," code for "marijauna smoker," should one not, or want to, know, is named after a section of the California penal code. Hence, 4:20 is a popular time for a smoke break. Or something to do on April twentieth. This may be obscure in a few years if not already. I've never been a skydiver.

Ralph Martin (1933-2005)
Roseburg National Cemetery

He was a nice guy
A man of generosity and integrity
Gone to be a guardian of his grandchildren.

Larry Sanstrums (1944-2005)
Lincoln Memorial Cemetery

Honorary mayor of Silver Lake

William Wilson (1964-2005)
Silver Lake Cemetery (Silver Lake)

Some people wade through life,
others pan for gold - Don's
in the middle of the stream,
splashing and looking under
all the rocks!
        Becky

Donald Keeling (1945-2005)
Grandview Cemetery

The Legendary
Gertrude Pollack
1918-2005
Sweet dreams, Mumsie

Gertrude Pollack (1918-2005)
Jacksonville Cemetery

US Marine Corps
A seedman dedicated to
Oregon and US agriculture

James Carne (1927-2005)
Union Hill Cemetery

An extravagant gesture of the Creator

165

G. William Rudberg Jr. (1943-2006)
Brush Prairie

Husband and father
Mentor and friend
Scholar and poet
Revolutionary and rabbinic inspiration

"My politics have not changed."

So read the simple blog entry by Stew Albert, co-founder of the Yippies, on January 28, 2006. Two days later, he died in his sleep at his home in Portland, Oregon, surrounded by his wife, Judy Albert; daughter, Jessica; and friends.

Stew Albert (1939-2006)
Havurah Shalom Cemetery

She lived so that the wild creatures
of the Earth,
including those in the ocean's depths,
would want to bless her.

Maxine McCloskey (1927-2006)
Lone Fir Cemetery (Portland)

Such an extraordinary desire for life
With so many reasons to quit

Daniel Taber (1948-2006)
Long Creek Cemetery

Your brilliance illuminates our souls,
Your humor lightens our spirits,
Your integrity resonates in our hearts forever

Joseph Gibbs II (1924-2006)
River View Cemetery

Making the world better

Ida Larson (1920-2007)
Greenwood Cemetery (Astoria)

Rodney brought a million good times and laughs. From
   his
"up and at 'em, rise and shine" to his "utscae overae
usterbae", he was the beginning and end to our best days.

166

There will be no replacement for his good cheer, jokes, not his comical grumpiness (bah humbug). Even now, he is singing "Good Night Irene the party is over" with a smile on
his face and a mischievous look. We miss you and love you.

Rodney Coate (1950-2008)
Glendale Cemetery

• • •

A family that pursued life with the strength, courage, and love taught to them by their mother Evelyn

Duncan
River View Cemetery

Among earliest interments Amity Cemetery

You'll note there are two Indian Jims recorded in this collection.

Indian Jim
Amity Cemetery

Came to Tillamook County in 1860; took a homestead 11 miles south of Tillamook City, cut a trail and packed his provisions to his cabin for five years. He lived in Tilla-mook County 48 years.

David Reasoner
Tillamook IOOF Cemetery

Crossed the plains in 1847, from Knox Co., Ill.

Settled in the Waldo Hills, where they resided until their deaths

Geer
Mount Hope Pioneer Cemetery

167

I have to say goodbye to you for now my friend
You were a humble giant you were a great friend
With a huge heart you taught me many things
I will wrestle with you again I will fish with you again
I'll see you again I know you are with me you travel
With me and you are part of who I am but we
All miss you
    Les Gutches

          Flack
          Miller Cemetery (Scio)

In memory of
Frank Tazewell Riddle
Native of Kentucky

Miner, rancher, frontiersman,
guide and interpreter during
the Modoc War, 1872-1873

Beloved husband of Winema

Dedicated by
Klamath County Historical Society
October 1985

          Frank Riddle
          Chief Schonchin Cemetery

In memory of
Ralph Dimmick
An all-American athlete, student, and man.
Whose [Notre Dame logo] was on
His heart
An athlete in the classroom a scholar on
The field, and everywhere a man.
Erected by the students of Notre Dame
University, in tribute to a memory they
Wish to perpetuate and hope to share.
R.I.P.

          Ralph Dimmick
          Hubbard Cemetery

In memory of
Winema, Modoc heroine
Interpreter for Peace Commission
Pensioned by Congress for courageous
and loyal service — Modoc War, 1872-3

Presented by Winema Chapter
Placed by Eulalona Chapter
Daughters of the American Revolution
May 30, 1932

They named a National Forest after this lady for her service and quick thinking during the ambush of the Peace Commissioners by Captain Jack and his followers. A native herself, she had the presence of mind to holler, "Soldiers coming!" in the native tongue just as one of the negotiators was about to be scalped, causing the Indian to drop his victim and scatter with the rest of the attackers into the lava beds.

Winema
Chief Schonchin Cemetery

I've learned from my Uncle Cliff
By Buddy Randle

I've learned from my Uncle Cliff to treasure and be proud
*   of your family.*
I've learned from my Uncle Cliff to treasure your friends
*   like they are your family.*
I've learned from my Uncle Cliff only Ford makes pick-up
*   trucks.*
He showed me how to turn a large goldfish into a very
*   large catfish.*
I've learned from my Uncle Cliff that you cannot retrieve
*   mail from the Palo Verde Post Office until a game of*
*   billiards is played over a cold Budweiser.*
He showed me not to let pain stop you from living.
I've learned to miss my Uncle Cliff.

A note attached to the tombstone. While not a true epitaph, it's nonetheless true.

Uncle Cliff
Belcrest Cemetery

Logger. Truck driver. Fighter. Opened & ran 1st bar in
Siletz for 38 years. An avid reader, he had an opinion on
everything: religion, politics, sex & history. Loved or

hated by all who knew him.

Leonard Whitlow
Pike-North Yamhill Cemetery

Naomi Pike Schenk
A kind and generous woman
Who survived the tragic
Donner Expedition
Arriving in California in 1847
This marker placed by
Marysville Parlor No. 162
Native Daughters Golden West.

Naomi Schenk
IOOF/GAR Cemetery (The Dalles)

Old Chief Ollicott, his sons Ta wa Toy and
Five Crows owned 3000 Cayuse horses.
Therefore Indians obtained the name of
Cayuse Tribe

Anon
Agency Mission Cemetery

Schonchin
Head Chief of the Modocs

His courageous loyalty to
his treaty obligations
kept the bulk of his tribe
from the warpath and
saved the Klamath settlements
1872-3
Marker erected by
Eulalona Chapter, D.A.R.
1932

Schonchin
Chief Schonchin Cemetery

The best crew chief a son could ever have.
I love you Dad
Sam Richardson #R13

Richardson
City View Cemetery

To serve his state and his people was to Frank Irvine a
beautiful adventure, a privilege without price, a responsi-
bility without limitations, a liberty too precious to be ap-
praised. In humble words and simple sentences he capital-
ized the human side of journalism.

Frank Irvine
Rose City Cemetery

U.S.M.C. 1945-49   572555
I.L.W.V. Local 21
Crew member
Kindergarten Cop
Point Break
Teenage Mutant Ninja III
Father of Consuelo, Ramona, Cody

Anon
Hudson Cemetery

We could almost hear the angels cheering as he crossed the
finish line! David was always laughter, energy and fun. He
was a great friend: caring and faithful. He was courageous
and always ready to encourage. He was passionate about
worship and serving Jesus, truly a "man after God's own
heart." We are so proud of him. We'll miss his infectious
laugh and his hugs. He is so loved!
    "Later"

David Newell
City View Cemetery

You were such a vibrant spirit
You who embraced life with such open loving exuberance
You delighted us with your quick wit
Touched us with your heart's warmth
You amazed us with your kaleidoscope of facial expres-
    sions
Revealing so well your flamboyant nature
You were a gift to us packaged brightly
Filled with warm and vivid memories
We love you

171

We miss you
We hold you close in our hearts

To catch a phrase
From Van's own use
Shines light on his very soul:
    "Gloriously wonderful"

Van
Oak Point Cemetery

FINAL TOUCHES
(POETICS)

The working title for this section was "Poetic and Philosophical" which was about as exciting as a ladies' tea. The entries are arranged alphabetically by first lines. I'm sure that many of them are "Borrowed" if I only knew their source. They are virtually all modern, so age ranking them would be fairly pointless. The fact that they are primarily modern says volumes about the cultural shift we've undergone at the turn of the millennium. For the most part they are cloaked in a mantle of grace, occasionally rustic. They can skirt close to "Enigmas" and dally with "Poignant."

A bright light begins to appear and the dawn is me, starting a new beginning.
  Nick Ferrer

> Nicholas Ferrer (1980-1998)
> Mountain View Memorial Gardens

A brother in the wind

> Steve Woodall (1944-2003)
> Applegate Pioneer Cemetery

A light in the channel
To guide you home

> Gene Schlappi (1934-1992)
> Greenwood Cemetery (Astoria)

A man rests here
  Who traveled far
Who plowed the dirt
  And roped a star
Who held them both
  In his rough hand
Stands again in his own land

> Emmet White (1907-1972)
> Monument Cemetery

A mother, a wife
A short lived life,
A daughter, a sister
We all shall miss her

An aunt, a niece,
Death brought her peace
A cousin, a friend
What seems so is not the end

She was a sweet, young lady
Who should have had years to live
The kind of person
That always has so much to give
She dedicated her life to her family
Whom without her seems so lost.
"Is this the price we must pay?" some might ask.
Yet, this situation is no such cost.
The truth, to tell you,
Neither I know why
Such a wonderful person,
So young, must die.
Yet, the only answer
That comes to mind
Is the one
Within these lines.
She lives in peace at last,
For her pain is forever gone.
Now she'll take care of others above
As here, we must go on.

Debra Toman (1955-1993)
Logan-Pleasant View Cemetery

A whisper away
A lady knows when to say goodbye

Donna Friton (1968-2004)
Adams Cemetery

Ali, you and Daddy come sit next to Grandmama
tell me all the Phenomenal things that you
desire, experience and remember

[on separate flush stone]

I AM phenomenal

I'll be back in two shakes

of a lamb's tail.

> Jody White (1960-2005)
> River View Cemetery

All men who go down to the sea in ships
To all seamen who have crossed the bar
On your eternal voyage beyond the north star
The sea was your life the mighty deep
They've just run eight bells
Now rest, now sleep

> Korry Jones (1966-2002)
> Sears Cemetery

All the things I've shared,
All the feelings I've bared,
   Were not wasted,
     nor thrown away,
  Instead they molded
     The me of today

> Donnalee Rose (1954-1990)
> Peaceful Hill Cemetery (Naselle)

Always wilderness bound

> Edmund Melton (1960-1985)
> Saint Wenceslaus Cemetery

And did you get what
you wanted from this life,
even so?
I did.
And what did you want?
To call myself beloved,
To feel myself beloved
on the earth.

> Francis Diskin (1947-2004)
> Mount Pleasant Cemetery

And God spoke the great Amen.

> Elisabeth Sarver (1948-2000)
> Bethel Lutheran Cemetery

Andrew swam with joy this rivers [sic] width,
And o'er its span he'd glide.
He lives in every swimmer's wake,
And in each runner's stride.

Andrew Nygaard (1982-1998)
Ocean View Cemetery

Before his eyes the horse and
Buggy became the space rocket

Ardath Schwab (1897-1998)
Franklin Butte Cemetery

Beloved of the
Rose sunset
Prays to Christ

Possessed with the
Bisons [sic] strength

Sweet Charlotte
Travels north with
The wild Cayuse
Far away

Where
memories and dreams
Are like
Thunder and lightning

Charlotte Walker (1924-1979)
Brown Cemetery (Beatty)

Beyond the rainbow new colors glow
In heavenly gardens and angle [sic] hair
Forever beautiful under Norman's care.

Norman Simonson Jr. (1957-1995)
Frank Abel Cemetery

Bold and brave a sailor true
He rest [sic] in peace above oceans blue

176

E. E. Clough, Capt. (1834-1903)
Sparta Cemetery

But one grain of sand
*   in the desert am I...*
Of what use would it be
*   for me to live and die*
If one of the shiniest grains
*   were not I?*

Karl Viacomte (1951-1977)
Stipp Cemetery

Child of Light
Bridge in the universe

So dearly loved

Danced in sunlight
Floated on moonbeams
Dreamed on clouds

Laughed soaring hawk songs
Cried brilliant rainbows
Reached for the stars

A boy who could pet bees
I love you Damie

Damien Parlor (1974-1984)
Idaho City Cemetery

Cruisin' the high road and joined a heavenly band

Billy Hammond (1940-1999)
Fairfield Cemetery

Dancer   Poet
*   Writer*

[on separate stone]

Grandma Wore Tights

Grandma wore tights in days gone by.

177

With stars in her eyes and show biz in her blood,
she lived life and loved people.

The people loved Grandma.
How she could dance across the stage
night after night with stars in her eyes.

Yes eyes.
The gaiety, the lights, the people were Grandma's life.
With the love of God she had it all together.
Now Grandma has found her paradise.

Elva Hull (1913-1999)
Ocean View Cemetery

Death is not extinguishing the candle.
It is putting out the light
Because dawn has come.

Frances Kaiser (1897-1987)
Saint Patrick's Historic Cemetery

Diane went home to be
with Jesus, the Master Painter.
You could hear Jesus say,
"Well done my faithful servant
Come and paint for me."

Diane McClure (1935-1995)
Cliffside Cemetery

Done plowing

M. J. Shell (1910-1990)
Bethany Pioneer Cemetery (Silverton)

1
Dor-o-thy four-
And Au-drey three-
Blue-eyed and sweet-
As they can be-
2
Two lit-tle sis-
Ters with fair hair-
They took to me-

178

Like a love-ly pair-
3
Here is the mes-
Sage the birds all bring-
Both of these lit-
Tle girls can sing!
4
They help their moth-
Er and scat-ter crumbs-
For the birds to eat-
When win-ter comes-
5
And then the birds-
Fly off to tell-
The whole world that-
They loved them well-
6
And that they look-
For them ev-er-y day-
When they come out-
With their dolls to play-
7
And high in the moun-
Tains where they live-
The fresh, sweet air-
Is sure to give-
8
Bright ros-y cheeks-
And health more and more-
to Au-drey three-
And Dor-o-thy four.

Written for Dorothy McKean
Myrtle Glenn Terry

Dorothy McKean Bowers (1925-1997)
Fir Grove Cemetery

embracing the end of a happy life
full circle, spin on

bite me

179

frogsguitardidjeridumotorcyclessunflowersthingsthat-
bouncedeepbellyla

Excerpt from freize around a bench. The words "bite me" are on the surface of the bench, discretely placed in one corner. I received an email from Timory's mother thanking me for my recognition of her daughter's memorial. She said it took some convincing of the staff at River View that it was an acceptable expression to write on a public marker.

Timory Hyde (1975-1997)
River View Portland

Fair Skies
Joyous flight

Gary Fletcher (1940-2000)
Willamette National Cemetery

Fly on proud bird, you're free at last

D. Ranney Munro III (1942-2000)
Camp Polk Cemetery

Folks in heaven don't do a thing
Walk streets of gold, play harp & sing.
I need a little house, flowers round the door
Children running in and out to bake some cookies.
Save your golden streets for those above
Satisfy my simple tastes with lots of folks to love.

Golda Miller
Lone Fir Cemetery (Portland)

Forever and for always he will be within our hearts
His gentle, loving manner setting him apart

He's walking through the forests now. He's camping in the trees
He's digging clams & hunting — his mind is now at ease

Many people loved him, his family and his friends
In his sentimental nature, we felt a love that never ends

As we look up to the heavens, we can almost see his face
Smiling and at peace in the warmth of Mom's embrace

Forever and for always, he will be a special part

*Of precious loving memories that we hold within our
   hearts*

   *Love,
   The Family*

> Scott Hall
> Peaceful Hill Cemetery

Friends, sit and shoot the breeze.

Chiseled into a granite bench top.

> Stephen Penner (1936-1998)
> Pine Grove Cemetery (Peoria)

*Gone fishing in
The river of life*

> Harold White (1921-2000)
> Willamette National Cemetery

*Gone to his dreamless bed.
Gone to his rest on high.*

> George Kelley (1867-1868)
> Cove Cemetery

Grace of God II

*Part of the human condition
is that my own death
will not concern me;
for others it will distress.
I shall lie in state of calmness,
and though with grief, they'll feel glad
that they can yet enjoy awareness.*
                    By Reba

> Reba (1912-2002)
> Mount Pleasant Cemetery (Seattle)

*Have you seen it first
   as a field of green
Watched it acquire a
   purplish sheen*

Seen it next as a waving
  sea of rust
To turn golden and
  revert to dust
    Don Smith

> Donald Smith (1921-1994)
> Mayville Cemetey

He had the eyes of
the eagle

> Darin Lawver
> Chief Schonchin Cemetery

He is walking in the shadows of our minds.

> Harold Horn (1921-1982)
> Desert Lawn Memorial

He planted trees where others dared not go.
"I wish I could paint with ease the landscape - green with
  fertile imaginings
only I can see, or let flow forth the bubbling spring of my
  own joy
in words of poetry."

> *from Tom's writings*

> Thomas Cribbins (1954-2008)
> Norway Cemetery

He smiled with us

> Carl Fenn (1978-1991)
> Boistfort Cemetery

Her life was a
work of heart

> Clara Foster (1924-2008)
> Eagle Point National Cemetery

Her simple life moves and inspires us
Just like waves beating against the rocky shore

> Ruth Lewis (1921-2010)

Here little Indian children played and here our children
*   played*
We farmed here and God blessed us

> Beryl (1921-2003) & Edna (1927-2008) Williams
> Midvale-Eastside Cemetery

Here we lie by consent, after 57 years 2 months and 2
days sojourning though life awaiting nature's immutable
laws to return us back to the elements of the universe, of
which we were first composed.

> James (1805-1887) & Elizabeth (1806-1889) Stephens
> Lone Fir Cemetery (Portland)

I am so wise
To think love will prevail
I am so wise

> Rebecca Schaeffer (1967-1989)
> Ahavai Shalom Cemetery

I go beyond the
realm of life
to see the truth

> Troy Kauffman (1968-2002)
> Stipp Cemetery

I have gone beyond the sunset
Will meet you over there someday

> Marie Dougherty (1922-1999)
> Bramlet Memorial Cemetery

I lived by a river
Just downstream
From God's place

> Jeanie Holmes (d. 2000)
> Pleasant Hill Cemetery (Pleasant Hill)

I miss you most of all when day is done

> Elthea (1915-1994) & Edwin (1909-1994) Barrett

I must go my friend is waiting

> Richard Jungwirth (b. 1940)
> Saint Mary Catholic Cemetery

I won't be far away, for life
goes on. Just listen with your
heart and you will hear, for my love
is always near Mike & Justin

> Karen Wammack (1971-2005)
> Elsie Cemetery

If I were a star way up in the sky then I could see ev-
erything that happened in the world. I wouldn't have to
read the newspapers or rely on what people say because
I'd only have to rely on my own eyes. Everyone would
be watching me and wondering "I wonder what it would
be like to be a star like her?" They would, late at night,
when all my friends and I are out twinkling in the sky, be
watching us and saying how gorgeous we are and thinking
what it would be like to be her.

> Holly Gay (1974-1990)
> City View Cemetery

If you need to talk
  I'll give you my ears.
If you need to cry
  I'll give you my shoulder.
If you need to laugh
  I'll give you my humor.
If you need to love
  I'll give you my heart.

> Rachel Bartlett (1971-1988)
> Mountain View Cemetery (Centralia)

I'll see ya, when I see ya!

> Shirley Moses (1937-2007)
> Idlewild Cemetery

In her white gown

We saw her shadow
Passing by the moon
Going up up up

Marilyn Ringering (1927-1993)
Robert Bird Cemetery

In life, oceans and continents kept grandfather John from
seeing and holding his namesake grandson, but now with
his passing, they are together at last and for all eternity.
Although they are gone, they are immortal as their spirits
join the clan ancestors to soar high above the braes and
glens and the lochs and crags of their beloved Scotland.
Listen very carefully and you will hear them singing amid
the skirl of the pipes as the wind howls over the heather in
the Scottish highlands.

John Bruce (1968-1972)
Union Point Cemetery

In our thoughts, in our greatest memories
Your love will live in our hearts forever.
"We promise you Mom… We will dance."

Melissa Compton (1967-2001)
Buxton Community Cemetery

In the winter of her life
She became as a child -
Giving her love freely,
Taking our love forever.

Ruth Myron (1909-1988)
United Church of Christ Cemetery (Ten O'Clock
Church)

It is almost impossible to
watch the ocean and not dream

Barbara (1948-1997)
Mount Calvary Catholic Cemetery

It is the climb, the exhilarating never ending climb

[verso]

185

"Rog"

He smiled, he climbed, he lived with intention.
He made the most of life... "Life is good!"
He aimed high — family, friends and mountains were his
*   life.*
"I am off to another summit!" he says.
God bless you, Robert — We will meet you at the top!

> Robert Stockhouse III (1972-2001)
> Greenwood Cemetery (Cathlamet)

It's all in a day in the bush with God

> Harry Pietrok (1937-1975)
> Saint Mary Catholic Cemetery

It's nightfall on the trail
My voice now still, encamped eternally
Underneath a stately tree
Atop this lovely hill

> Hershel Tanzer (1926-2003)
> Ahavai Shalom Cemetery

It's okay, Mom, we'll catch up

> Jerry Noyes (1984-2002)
> Confederated Tribes of Grand Ronde Cemetery

Just as I am

> Lawrence Burr (1939-1987)
> Bunker Hill Cemetery

Ke kane i aloha i ka aina a me ka moana
Mai ka wekiu a hiki i lalo loa o ke kai

The man who loved the land and the ocean
From the top of the mountain to the bottom of the sea

> Christopher Pelfrey (1967-1993)
> Forest Lawn Cemetery (Gresham)

La vita é bella

> Emma Howell (1981-2001)

186

Laughing, running, shy,
Her shoe's [sic] are empty now.
But our heart's [sic] will be
Filled with her memory forever.

Colleen Porter (1969-1986)
Cambridge Cemetery

Let me live in a house by the side of the road and be a
friend to man.

Harry (1915-1998) & Carol (b. 1940) Neely
Mountain View Cemetery (Centralia)

Let our spirits wander over the hills
We loved so well
And in this spot forever may God let
our spirits dwell

Robert (1898-1982) & Emma (1900-1973) Jenkins
Cascade Locks Cemetery

Lo, I am with you always
Free... like the winds

Roberta Ellerbroek (1935-1986)
Mountain View Memorial Gardens

Look up, my loves, above the trees; I'm up here now,
please wave to me. The Angels here, hug me now, they
kiss my cheek, caress my brow. The pain down there, so
plain to see, only happy things are here for me,
that much I know. You must not cry and must not fear;
wipe your eyes and dry your tears.
I love you and you love me. But look up here at me,
I'm free, With Him, I'll wait for thee. Oh, look up,
my loves, and you will see the beautiful wings He gave
to me.

John Roberts (1940-1998)
Lebanon Odd Fellows and Masonic Cemetery

Love makes all the difference
In the way we view a day

It can paint our lives with rainbows
It can chase the blues away
It can comfort when we're little
It can touch us when we're grown
It can give such sweet serenity
At times we are alone

Love makes all the difference
In the way we choose to live
For the more we freely give away
The more we have to give
It's the joy of our existence
From the moment of our birth
As long as we have love
We have the greatest gift on Earth

I found a reference to this poem on Google, but because the photo from which the poem was extracted was no longer available, I couldn't tell if it was from a separate source or the same tombstone.

Homer (1896-1987) & Jennie (1899-1988) Wolf
Crescent Grove Cemetery

Loved watching sports   *Loved eating chocolate*

Thank you for touching my life and enjoying how I
touched yours. Thank you for returning my smiles and
laughter. Thank you for looking past my disability and
seeing the person that I was inside. Thanks you to my im-
mediate and extended family members for loving me with
all of your hearts and showering me with so much of your
happiness. I will see all of you someday in heaven.

Life is always better when you share your kindness
And leave others happier than you found them in.

Michael Parker (1989-2003)
Lone Fir Cemetery (Portland)

Loving Memories

Your gentle face and patient smile
With sadness we recall
You had a kindly word for each

And died beloved by all.
The voice is mute and stilled the heart
That loved us well and true
Ah, bitter was the trial to part
From one so good as you.
You are not forgotten loved one
Nor will you ever be,
As long as life and memory last
We will remember thee.

Eugene Tracy (d. 1972)
Westside Cemetery

Loving wife, devoted mother, cherished friend
Wings a mile long carried the bird away

Laurie Hollander (1951-2002)
Havurah Shalom Cemetery

Mark was here, but now he's gone;
He left his name to carry on.
Those who knew him, knew him well;
And those who did not, farewell.

Mark Zamora Jr. (1979-2004)
Columbian Cemetery

Mo playing the eternal
Gig in heaven

Morris Perry Jr. (1952-2004)
Roseburg National Cemetery

Mom
Follow your sunbeam
Be with your son
We'll meet you in heaven
When our work is done

Harriett Smith (1937-2006)
Oakville Cemetery

Movin' on

Dave Clemmons (1926-1990)
Sunnyside Chimes Memorial Garden

189

Music speaks where words fail

> Joseph Ash (1916-2004)
> Eugene Masonic Cemetery

My anchor holds

> Henry Williams (1920-2002)
> Willamette National Cemetery

Never shall I leave the places that I love
Never shall they go from my heart
Even though my eyes
Are somewhere else

> Anon
> Taft Cemetery

No more logs do I pull
No more whistles do I hear
With my Savior now I rest
A yarder engineer

> Virgil Campion (1913-1986)
> Masonic Cemetery (Canyonville)

Now he sails a different sea.

> Charles "Bearfoot Charlie" Hollis (1907-1984)
> American Legion Cemetery

Now they lay me down to sleep
I'm buried at my grandpa's feet
But we're not here, make no mistake
We're fishing in heaven, with heavenly bait.
Meet me at
The River of Life

> Robert Holbrook (1972-1990)
> Valley View Cemetery

Off on another adventure

> Dennis Owre (1955-1994)
> Saint Patrick's Historic Cemetery

On the Oregon Trail
to Heaven

> Linda Conklin-Hand (1958-2003)
> Lyle-Balch Cemetery

On the road again!

> Adolf (1925-1995) & Loretta (b. 1933) Amstand
> Cliffside Cemetery

On voudrait revenir a la page ou on aime
Mais la page ou on meurt est déja sous vos doigts

Would that you could return to the page where you love,
But the page where you die is already under your fingers.

> Herbert (1898-1969) & Emma (1908-1992) Bara
> Saint Barbaras Cemetery

Onward ever,
Lovely river,
Softly calling to the sea,
Time, that scars us,
Maims and mars us,
Leaves no track or trench on thee.

Excerpt from poem, "Beautiful Willamette," by the deceased. Story has it that Sam was going down to the river to cast himself in and commit suicide when he was overcome by the beauty of the river and wrote this poem instead. The Columbia River belongs to the entire Territory, but the Willamette belongs only to the Kingdom of the Willamette, a small principality completely surrounded by the United States.

> Sam Simpson (1845-1899)
> Lone Fir Cemetery (Portland)

Operation Desert Storm
Operation Iraqi Freedom - KIA - POW
507th Maintenance Co.

I would lay down my life for my family and nation if
it was worth it, and this one is to let them appreciate
the taste of their freedoms. Freedom isn't free and some-
one must do what they must do to preserve it. The Bible
states, "Blessed is he who lays down his life for the sake
of his friends." I fear not and am motivated by the fear of
the unknown and being a part of the bigger picture. What-

ever doesn't kill you will make you stronger.

It should be pointed out that Donald didn't choose his epitaph.

> Donald Walters (1969-2003)
> Restlawn Cemetery (Salem)

Our lives are like sand
falling through the hour
glass washing on the shore.

> Neal Swigost (1980-1993)
> Sandy Ridge Cemetery

our mom
spirits mingling among dreams
reminds us of a loving mom
resting not our mom
she is free in the breeze
summer and winter

> Anon
> Damascus Cemetery

Pilot tower
Coming home

> Robert Plympton (1916-2003)
> Willamette National Cemetery

Pioneer

His mansion
a tent
under a
juniper tree

> Silas Kilgore (1915-1997)
> Bonanza Cemetery

Raised on
Corn bread, beans and a lot of love

> Margaret Fisher (1915-1991)
> Pleasant Hill Cemetery (Pleasant Hill)

Resting in hopes of a glorious resurrection

Christian Berthold (1899-1916)
Emanuel Lutheran Cemetery

Ride with me and you will see
a great journey meant to be
you can hold my hand, take a ride
on the white horse called "Victory"
see my face, jump on board
everything I promised will unfold
wave good-bye to the people you loved
on to paradise, on the wings of a dove
how can I delight you, king of kings
just have faith and see my faith off we go, hold
on tight let your sweet spirit take flight
your families will learn that you still live
your spirit soaring high, safe and brave
so ride with me and you will see
"a soul searching for eternity"

Michele Andrews (1965-1998)
Crescent Grove Cemetery

rock
sand
ocean
strength
memory
love

Maurice Georges (1921-2002)
Beth Israel Cemetery

S. T. Jackson is my name
America is my nation
Salem is my stopping place
And heaven, my destination

S. T. Jackson (1898-1952)
Waverly Memorial Cemetery

Sacred
to
the memory of Ann
Eliza Calvert, who
died the 21st of Dec.

1857 in her 19th year
saying I suffer much
but one moment in
glory will pay for
all

> Ann Calvert (1838-1857)
> Rock Creek Cemetery

Say, Joe, will you tell me where
you've been, with a twinkle in
your eye & a lopsided grin?
"I've been ropin' & ridin' &
fishin' with my friends,"
Well, Joe, will you tell me where
you'll go from here?
"To the rivers, to the streams,
to the mountains of my dreams —
anywhere my wings will take
me — to the place where life
begins."

> Joseph Douglas (1968-1990)
> Lebanon Odd Fellows and Masonic Cemetery

See you at the crossroads

> Michael Ashline (1979-1996)
> Gresham Pioneer Cemetery

She was like a child, holding
our blessed mother's hand

> Judith Esther (1964-2005)
> Hudson Cemetery

She's dancing a dance of love
In the Garden of Life

> Nancy Walsh (1932-2005)
> Skyline Memorial

So much to do, so little time.

> Ryan Westerman (1980-1998)
> Woodville Cemetery

194

Some people come into our lives
and quickly go

Some stay for awhile
and leave footprints on our hearts

and we are never, ever the same

Robert Donnelly (1934-1999)
Oswego Pioneer Cemetery

Song of Sherwood
(In the Days of Old)
By Ken Ford

Deep in the heart
of the Sherwood I know
Livin and lovin
is all that she knows
Nestled in the valleys
of Oregon she grows
Railroads and sawmills
and farms she will grow.

Chorus: Oh mighty you be
but small that you are
Sherwood you're my home
I no longer roam.

Pain and sorrow
and loss we have known
Loved ones gained
and loved ones lost
Churches were built
and fellowships were formed
Freedom to worship
and worship we did.

Sherwood wasn't built in a day
it took the likes of Robin
and his merry ole men
Men of renown

and women of great strength
They carved out a town
and she's a hundred years old.

> Ken Ford (1950-2003)
> Pleasant View Cemetery

Storms all weathered and life's seas crossed

> Frank Fuquay (1919-1986)
> North Cemetery

Such sweet memories
With time sorrow yields... A.A.I.

This, evidently, is a quote, but I haven't figure out who A. A. I. is nor whence the poem. Could A. A. I. be an Imholt?

> Betty (b. 1927) & Patrick (1918-1991) Imholt
> Saint Patrick's Historic Cemetery

Tethered to earth's security
Ah, but with wings to soar!
May this be ever your legacy
What could I wish you more?

> Caroline Smith
> Mount Pleasant Cemetery (Seattle, WA)

Tending the flowers in heaven

> Annie Munro (1904-1997)
> Yamhill-Carlton Cemetery

Thanks for stopping by.

> Donald (b. 1926) & D. (1927-1997) Lovell
> Gotcher Cemetery

The little bird is truly free.

> Katrina Weter (1970-2006)
> Cox Pioneer Cemetery

The fish are rising
children are laughing with joy
Bon's free and at peace

The grass grows thinner here my son. This path found
in childhood, the field no longer bends freely with the
wind: distant field we knew, far away. What was it you
said? "God's country?" Once maybe, now domain of man.
The birds no longer fly here. Gone. The murmuring
song of life, the river now a trickle, muddy water.
Sadly so, I'm happy for your sleep. This paradise
once yours. It's [sic] memory would make you weep.

Donald Stanhope (1959-1984)
Woodbine / Green Mountain Cemetery

The morning's here. Another day
The sun is shining through.
I left my worries all behind,
Today, I start anew.

Lois (b. 1931)
Moon Creek Cemetery

The movements
of birds and trees
carry the song
of our lives forward

Not departure
but a voyage done!

Joseph (1911-1997) & Frieda (b. 1914) Canvel
Lane Memorial Gardens

The reflection of your life
has helped us to see
more deeply into ourselves
and the one's [sic] we love

Anon
Fort Rock Cemetery

The ride never ends Dad

Wilbur Milford (1917-2007)
Roseburg National Cemetery

197

The rolling stone
Stops here[,] our friend

> Fred Winkler (1932-2007)
> Roseburg National Cemetery

The rose will bloom again

> Rose Lawvor (1919-1960)
> Chief Schonchin Cemetery

The stars are a
flyers [sic] rosary

> Frank Stratton (1905-1994)
> Fort Rock Cemetery

Their latest
Adventure in awareness

> Ann (1927-1992) & Richard (1926-1993) Smith
> Masonic Cemetery (St. Helens)

There is no higher league now.
I have achieved it all. I'm playing
On God's winning team. Don't worry
I won't fall. There is no greater
Team work or sportsmanship about.
There's never any foul balls and
No one is ever out. I'll still live
Here through you Mom — you'll
Never be alone, for several times
Throughout your life I'll be
Sliding into home.

Three point master

> Randal Cunningham (1984-1998)
> Mountain View Cemetery (Centralia)

Think of me when blue birds fly
And sun tinged clouds line the sky
If my parting has left a void
Then fill it with remembered joy
My life's been full. I savored much

Friends. Good times. A loved ones touch

> Ruth (b. 1922) & Selby (1917-1994) Weaver
> Island City Cemetery

This is not the end;
not even the beginning of the end;
but, perhaps, the end of the beginning.

> Tara Ostrom (1941-2004)
> Miller Cemetery

This warrior and his wife, their race on Earth now run
Now sleep with the Great Spirit in the earth and sky and
> *sun*

> Douglas (1933-1996) & Gwen (1933-1995) Gribble
> Gribble Cemetery

This warrior's spirit now rests
with the Great White Buffalo

> Frederick Mink (1929-1999)
> Grandview Cemetery

Though we were very close to each other
We each had our own lives and own goals
We were together always in our hearts
A relationship based on love and individualism

> Thomas (1942-1986) & Diana (b. 1943) Kruse
> River View Cemetery

Though your smile is gone forever, your laugh I cannot
> *hear*
Your hand I cannot touch[,] I'll never lose the memory
For the one I love so much.
If love could've saved you
You would've never died

> Joshua O'Neal (1979-1997)
> United Church of Christ Cemetery (Ten O'Clock
> Church)

Till tomorrow comes

> Ellis (1925-2002) & Bettee (b. 1929) Gerdes

To light one candle to help one child to see
A star in the sky; to sing high, high, high
To sing along with me.

Melinda-Heather
Bay City IOOF Cemetery

To Mom

When the daphne blooms in springtime,
And your roses all unfurl,
I'll see you in your garden,
As though you were a girl.
You'll be tending to your flowers,
To chase the winter gloom.
I'll see you in the springtime,
When the daphne starts to bloom.

Irene Bancroft (1921-2003)
Multnomah Park Cemetery

Un amour perdu
Un amour rêve
Un amour dansant
Un amour odscurci [sic]
Un amour terrestre
    Fin
       d'amour

A lost love
A dream of love
A dancing love
A hidden love
An earthly love
  The end
    of love

"Odscurci" is a misspelling of "obscurci."

Robert Shultz (1953-1985)
Oakville Cemetery

Walks with nature
In the wind

Marlene Wilcox (1931-2005)
Roseburg National Cemetery

We are not afraid of tomorrow
For we have seen yesterday
And we love today

Nelson (1924-2005) & Myrtle (1927-2003) Brockman
Monroe Cemetery

We shall
Meet at the river...

Beverlee Neider (1936-1998)
Cambridge Cemetery

We will meet again in
The winners circle

James Faust (1939-2003)
Roseburg National Cemetery

We'll talk to those we love
From tumbling mountain streams
And whisper guiding thoughts
From treetops high above

Bernard (1917-1993) & Lillian (1918-2004) Douglass
Tualatin Plains Presbyterian Church Cemetery

When you were born, you cried,
but we rejoiced. You lived your life
in such a way, that when you died,
we all cried, and you rejoiced.

Bernice Foley (1975-1995)
Fairfield Mennonite Church Cemetery

Who lived, laughed and loved
You decorated my life

[verso]

May your time
be filled with
relaxing sunsets,

cool drinks and
sand between
your toes.
     Friend forever

> Tammy Fowler (1971-2006)
> Oak Hill Cemetery

Yet shall there live on
Your noble dreamlike spirit
And may the essence of your
Dreams endure with radiance
For infinity

> William Fischman (1902-1990)
> Neveh Zedek Cemetery

You have passed your time on earth
   Gentle soul
Touched many lives
   Gentle soul
You helped me live, helped me grow
There's one thing you should know
How much you mean to me
   Gentle soul

You fought the fight, ran the race
No one can ever take your place
I love you forever
   Gentle soul

> Clow MacKey (1905-1995)
> Cascade Locks Cemetery

STOP, YOU'RE KILLING ME
(HUMOR)

Most epitaph collections fall into one of two categories: those of famous people or humorous ones. The marble forests have been cruised for the bizarre and the sublime. How much work morticians must go through getting those tongues unstuck from those cheeks. It's understandable, some epitaphs are downright funny, if not all intentionally.

A better wife than her husband deserved.
A better mother than her children deserved.

> Margaret Fry (1929-2006)
> Blooming Cemetery

A gentle giant - with attitude

> Gilbert Hager (1980-2000)
> Sandy Ridge Cemetery

A naval aviator who never got lost...
...hardly ever.

> William Walters (1905-1987)
> Joseph Cemetery

A Texan by birth
An Oregonian by choice

> James Gaines (1914-1982)
> Paisley Cemetery

A Gaelic poet sang...
It is no joy without Clan Donald,
It is no strength to be without them.

> John MacDonald (1929-2004)
> Sunset Cemetery (Ontario)

All dressed up and no place to go

> Charlo Dick (1953-2006)
> Brainard Cemetery

Always go to other people's funerals. Otherwise they

won't go to yours.
  Yogi Berra

> Mathew Beecher (1952-2001)
> Tualatin Plains Presbyterian Cemetery

Barbara stopped here

> Barbara Lockwood (1944-2007)
> Joseph Cemetery

Beloved sister to women and dogs

> Cassondra Brown (1985-2003)
> Portland Memorial Mausoleum

Blessed are those who clean up

> Anon
> Coles Valley Cemetery

Builder of tall buildings or catching catfish
He lived life & is loved by so many

> Arvest Bacon (1936-2000)
> Valley View Cemetery

Catch ya later

> James Jeffries (1962-2003)
> Canyon Hill Cemetery

Chuckawalla Sam

> Samuel Mandeville (1896-1974)
> Paisley Cemetery

Deal me in

> Gilbert Kern (1928-2002)
> Willamette National Cemetery

Death is a journey
And you know how I like to travel

> Alma Markee (d. 1984)
> St. Mary Catholic Cemetery

Do not disturb

Taking a nap

> Anon
> Condon Cemetery

Don't cry[,] Mom
I'm fine
It's only money

> Timothy Wilke (1973-2004)
> Finley-Sunset Hills Cemetery

Don't take no talent to get old
Just hang around while you unfold
But who should ever live so long
If all they ever did was wrong?
Or who'd survive time's awesome flight
If all they ever did was right?
Lucky me I wasn't shot
Just prematurely went to pot

> Alois Deggendorfer (1898-1982)
> Damascus Cemetery

Don't worry the party won't start without me

> Christy Wilson (1978-1999)
> Riddle Cemetery

Excavating on higher ground

> James Staven
> Pleasant View Cemetery

Fish on

> Neal Davidson Jr. (1931-2003)
> Willamette National Cemetery

For God, Country, and Old Wazzu

> David Williams (d. 1922)
> Phillips Cemetery

God bless
Everyone I've
Ever known

Loved, or
Disliked

> Mary Hoover (1930-2002)
> Riverview Cemetery (Boardman)

God couldn't be
Everywhere so He
Created grandparents

> Jack (1920-2009) & Nellie (1920-1995) Nunnellee
> Redmond Memorial Cemetery

Gone fishing
with Missy

> Duane Jones (1930-2008)
> Eagle Point National Cemetery

Gone for the bait

> Mildred Long (1931-1993)
> Cliffside Cemetery

Gone shopping

> Bernadette Digges (1947-2003)
> Woodville Cemetery
> —
> Connie White (1974-2005)
> Buxton Cemetery

Gone to catch the big one

> Rusty Purvis (1962-2002)
> Ironside Cemetery

Gone to happy hour

> Thomas Sampson (1929-2007)
> Roseburg National Cemetery

Gone to prepare a place
For you. Be back soon
   Love[,] Jesus

> Cleveland Brown (1966-2001)
> Sparlin Cemetery

He ministered   She prayed

Don't ask me why I find this funny.

> Ila (1910-1991) & Kermit (b. 1909) Riegelmann
> Mountainside Cemetery

He never met a stick he didn't like
"There's no such thing as a bad piece of wood."

> Dean Gordanier Sr. (1918-1995)
> Columbia Pioneer Cemetery

Heck of a deal

> Robert Paterno (1930-2007)
> Lookingglass Cemetery

Here lies a town girl who became
*   a ranchers wife and right hand*
A passionate mother. A lover of
*   family*
A promoter of womens education
*   and a shopper*
Knew I would be asked
*   Yes Honey I will get the gate*

> Anon
> Long Creek Cemetery

I have made many trades in my life,
But I think I went in the hole on this one.

> Fred Barnard (1918-1993)
> Ridgefield Cemetery

I have three wonderful sons, It's too bad you couldn't keep
*   me a little longer.*

> Edith Porter (d. 2000)
> Kesser Israel Cemetery

I told the doctors
I was just fine!

Don't pass the entry by with noticing the name.

Joy Makin (1928-2010)
Yachats Memorial Park

I told you I was sick

Gloria Martin (1926-2002)
Robert Bird Cemetery

This is showing up around the country often enough to qualify as a "Palliative."

I wouldn't miss my only chance
For omnipotent enlightenment

Rachael Burchard (1921-2004)
South Yamhil Cemetery

I'd rather be shopping at Nordstroms

Patricia (1928-2003)
Lone Oak Cemetery

I'm going to miss me

Porter Payne (1921-2005)
Union Cemetery (Union)

In loving memory of
Paul Eyman
Who never sat around much

Paul Eyman
Smyrna Cemetery

In the upper room

Bernice Burns (1883-1959)
River View Cemetery

It's a good day to poke some holes in the sky.

Under an etching of a small, personal airplane.

William (1956-2005) & Christi (b. 1960) Bonfield
Rock Point/Gold Hill IOOF Cemetery

It's always something

Jan Peckham (1946-1999)

208

Union Cemetery (Cedar Mills)

It's your mother

Mary Ogden (1920-2000)
Odd Fellows Cemetery (Dayton)

*Ive [sic] done all my traveling
And decided to settle down here*

William Bennett (b. 1922)
Pine Haven Cemetery

Keep the pot hot Dad

Elmer Simmons (1892-1978)
Antioch Cemetery

*Last load delivered
to heaven*

Accompanied by an engraving of a dump truck plus trailer.

Dan Yoder (1954-1996)
Jacksonville Cemetery

Life is uncertain. Eat dessert first.

Richard (1940-2005) & Colleen (b. 1941) Dohrn
Ocean View Cemetery (Warrenton)

Loved in spite of himself

Bob Mabry (1923-2000)
Willamette National Cemetery

*Loving husband forever
And two weeks*

James Kane (1941-2000)
Willamette National Cemetery

*May you be in
heaven an hour
before the
devil
knows you're
dead*

Irish Toast

> Brian Reilly (d. 2005)
> Kelly Cemetery

May your days be sunny
And the elk slow and fat

> William Casey (1921-2004)
> Summerville Cemetery

Mayor
of Haines

Office upstairs

> William Lee (1903-1975)
> Haines Cemetery

Mother gave All Ten of us,
"Unforgetable Moments."
We weren't ready for her
to leave. God said, time
to rest no more mashed
potatoes and gravey. [sic]

> Marjorie Borns (1918-2008)
> Arivaca Cemetery (Arizona)

Now giving
Tours of heaven

> Fred & Yuton (1927-2000) Benton
> Willamette National Cemetery

Off like a herd of turtles

> Richard Gainer (1923-2000)
> Willamette National Cemetery

Old rock hounds never die
They petrify

Next to a hunk of petrified wood.

> Orvan Hatfield (1913-1996)
> Idlewild Cemetery

On the edge of passing days

I rather thought Paradise would be like a library

Times Arrow
Decendant of Chief Huckswelt
Weelapa Tribe of the Chinook's [sic]

Death will always come out of season

> Edward Nielsen (1961-1997)
> Bay Center Cemetery

On the highway to heaven [his]
Drive like hell and you'll get there [hers]

> Herman (d. 1986) & Agnes (d. 1992) Baxter
> Mount Calvary Catholic Cemetery (Portland)

One of the good ones

> H. J. Howard (1925-2006)
> Antioch Cemetery

Oregon or bust

> Katherine (1911-1998) & Herbert (1908-2000) Justen
> Buck Hollow Cemetery

People are like flowers.
It has been a pleasure
walking in your garden

> Donald Jagoe (1930-2005)
> Pilot Butte/Greenwood Cemetery

Plop plop
fizz fizz
Oh what a relief it is

> Eino Kangas (1932-1994)
> Union Cemetery (Union)

Pop, we are sharing.

> Raymond Wilson (1896-1952)
> Brumbaugh Cemetery

Raised four beautiful daughters
with only one bathroom and
still there was love

> Theodore (1931-2008) & Nedine (1932-1997) Barn-
> house
> Mitchell Cemetery

Sam Shattuck was
hung by mistake

What do you mean, it's not funny?

> Stan Shattuck
> IOOF Cemetery (Coburg)

Save the pieces!
I can fix it.

Over an etching of a VW Beetle.

> Anon
> Valley View Cemetery (Vale)

See ya later

> Scott Banke (1989-2001)
> Evergreen Memorial Cemetery

See you at the house

> Grace Prokop (1921-2004)
> Dallas Cemetery

See you soon, maybe tomorrow...

> Arthur Conrad (1947-1998)
> Mountain View Cemetery (View, WA)

See you tomorrow

> Larry Hatteberg (1942-1985)
> Valley View Cemetery

She loved maters and taters
and us kids

> Johnnie Crum (1900-1996)
> Forest Lawn Cemetery (Gresham)

so many cars, so little time

> H. Willard Smith (1926-1997)
> River View Cemetery (Portland)

Sold

> Henry Walpin (1921-2000)
> Willamette National Cemetery

"The fruit peddler"
A Christian man

> Fred DeSimone (1938-2006)
> Sparlin Cemetery

The only way
to fly.

Western Airlines slogan.

> Frances Cummings (1907-1985)
> Mount Pleasant Cemetery (Seattle, WA)

The phone must be for you
Smile

> Kristie Pergin (1976-1992)
> Woodville Cemetery

They said she was too different
and she wrote too many tunes

> Alice Spear (1923-1989)
> Coos River Cemetery

This pig has flown

> Florence Lussier (1948-2006)
> Washougal Memorial Cemetery

This wasn't in my schedule book

> Anon
> Lone Fir Cemetery (Portland)

Through the lips

Over the tounge [sic]
Look out tummy
Here it comes

> Walter Borns (1913-1975)
> Arivaca Cemetery (Arizona)

Tree hugger
"left town" 1999

> Jim Everts (1940-1999)
> Aumsville Cemetery

Tried to leave the woodpile a little higher than we found
it.

> Claude (b. 1922) & Frances (1923-1998) Friend
> Scottsburg Cemetery

Umpiring with God now

> V. L. Cooper (1933-1998)
> Kinder Cemetery

We miss you so very much, Mommy, but we'll be home
soon.
We know you'll leave the light on!

> Jane Dowd (1918-1998)
> Saint Mary's Cemetery (Corvallis)

We woke up at the Pearly Gates

> Destiny Maitland (1998-2006)
> Forest Lawn Cemetery (Gresham)

Well, I'm only curious

> Esther Lyon (1914-2002)
> Silverton Cemetery

Where did the time go

> Lois Baker (1936-2000)
> North Palestine Cemetery

Where the sidewalk ends...
True life begins.

"What the hell...?"

> Glen Myers (1980-1999)
> Fairview Cemetery (Ontario)

Who should live so long?

> Gertie Bunnell (1912-1983)
> Estacada IOOF Cemetery

With the Lord, enjoying a good cup of Yuban

> Robin Boon (1913-2004)
> Aumsville Cemetery

You put your right foot in

> Dawn Vocé (1954-2004)
> Stearns Cemetery

You're on your own [his]
Not any more [hers]

> Seymour (d. 1990) & Edith (d. 1994) Lehman
> Havurah Shalom Cemetery

You're welcome here
Have a seat
If I was home I'd
Make you something to eat

> Frank Berry (1932-2000)
> Valley View Cemetery

215

Death Is Always Out of Season
(Poignancies)

Death is not always sorrowful. Sometimes it's okay; it comes at the right time. Sometimes it's a blessed relief. Sometimes it is a grievous error, a cosmic mistake. Sometimes it's hard to accept the perfection of a world gone mad. How did it get this way? This is the part of the collection that's difficult to deal with. These are the short stories that will fell you to your knees. Too often the age is too young. Much too young. But as I'm fond of saying (never quote yourself!), these are chili peppers for the soul; they burn but they make life all the more precious.

Some entries only spotlight untimely deaths, but others go far beyond that. You should be warned, some are too painful to bear.

> *A child is like a butterfly in the wind. Some can fly higher*
> *than others.*
> *But each one flies the best it can. Why compare one*
> *against the other.*
> *Each one is different. Each one is special. Each one is*
> *beautiful.*

Abigail Wheat (2002)
Sunnyside Chimes Memorial Gardens

> *A flower just blooming into life*
> *Enticed an angel's eye*
> *"Too pure for earth," He said*
> *"Come home"*
> *And bade the flouerette die*

Amanda Cichosz (1983-2002)
IOOF Memorial Cemetery (Woodland)

> *A little baby girl*
> *So tiny, so new*
> *Terrible things happen*
> *And we wonder why they do*

> *Your silky dark hair*
> *Your soft pink skin*
> *You race through our minds*
> *Again and again*

> *We ask ourselves questions*

Questions like how and why
We try not to break down
But we always seem to cry

We ask God why
Because we had not much time with you
It doesn't seem fair
But these things never really do
    Your sister Melissa

Zalena Masterson (2002-2002)
High View Cemetery

Adieu, Mother, adieu.

Betty Hutton (1923-1998)
Mount Calvary Catholic Cemetery

AIDS took our life
But not our love
    We won

David (1951-1994) Benton & Scott (1956-1996) Steele
Lone Fir Cemetery (Portland)

Alone among many

Theodosia Lewis (1910-1979)
Coos River Cemetery

Assassinated Dec. 6, 1941

Merlin Chooktoot (1920-1941)
Brown Cemetery (Beatty)

Born in heaven
Not on earth

Another palliative which happened to sneak into this mournful lot.

Joseph Wisdom (1989-1989)
Yamhill-Carlton Cemetery

Catholic Relief Services
Cambodia - Egypt - Yemen

He crossed his Rubicon

218

Stephen Nicholls (1949-1982)
Gethsemani Catholic Cemetery

Chosin Few

The battle of the Chosin Reservoir in the Korean War was a particlarly harsh conflict in the dead of winter, where the UN forces were outnumber 2-to-1, but managed to break out of the Chinese blockade, nonetheless. Veterans of the battle are known as the Chosin Few.

Milton Lockner (1931-2002)
Willamette National Cemetery

Come Mamma

Emily Marsh (1875-1876)
Forest View Cemetery

Dad and son lie side by side.
They wanted to live, they wanted to give.
They had great days together.
Just not enough years.

Dennis Dillon (1951-2001)
Buck Hollow Cemetery

Died under operation

B. Maziretzky (1892-1900)
Ahavai Shalom Cemetery

Don't be scared, Jesus wif us okay.

Alec Thurston (1995-2002)
Canyon Hill Cemetery

Enlisted in Co. C, 34 Ia. Inft.
Died in the service Jan. 20, 1863.
He sleeps in an unknown grave
in the National Cemetery
Memphis, Tenn

Mary (1833-1913) & Matthew (1833-1863) Harbison
Lafayette Pioneer Cemetery

For a good dad
Have fun in heaven

James Church Jr. (1960-1998)
Buxton Cemetery

For a little while

David Nolen (1978-1978)
Camp Polk Cemetery

God's Littlest Cowboy

He's drawn a horse from Satan's herd
A black bronc that's never be spurred.
He gripped the rein and nodded his head
Called for the beast who's [sic] eyes glowed red.
The chute gate sprung then sailed wide open
To ride for 8 seconds he was prayin' and hope'n.
With the first jump that horde breathed fire
And the next three it kicked even higher.
Tossed its head squealed and blowed
Threw a wild horse fit, 'cause it knew it was rode.
When the whistle sounded he fanned the beast
And in its eyes that fire ceased.
You see that horse was life, the cowboy our son
And the ride he made was like no other one.
The truest of champions and hero and joy
And always he'll be God's Littlest Cowboy.

Tyrell Clark (1994-1994)
Canyon City Cemetery

Gold and silver have I none
But worth a "million" is my son

Cary Mauch (1955-1970)
Ilwaco Cemetery

Gone so soon

Lawrence Claypool (1881-1881)
Camp Polk Cemetery

He disliked emotion
not because he felt
lightly, but because
he felt deeply

220

Kyle Potter (1942-1995)
Riddle Cemetery

He faltered by the wayside, and
the angels took him home.

James Sutherlin (1867-1874)
Valley View Cemetery (Sutherlin)

He gave us charm to gladden us
Although his days were brief
We have lovely memories
As solace for our grief

Troy Sullivan (1974-2000)
Valley Memorial Cemetery

He loved the woods... And there he died

Ernest Schoenborn (1941-1984)
Mollala Memorial Cemetery

Heaven doesn't seem
so far away
Since little Jim
went there to stay.

Anon
Pilot Butte/Greenwood Cemetery

Her last words:

Oh Mother I hear the
Angels singing and they
Sing for you Mother

Norad Coffin (1872-1889)
Union Cemetery (Union)

Her last words were do
the girls know I am
going away

This is the epitaph which started my collection. Arguably, the saddest short story I know. Or, is that the shortest sad story that I know?

221

Olive Wren (1871-1881)
Cornelius United Methodist Cemetery

Here lies…
A secret waiting
    to be told
A treasure waiting
    To be found
And a mother's
    wish come true

Evan Mason (1990-1996)
Comstock Cemetery

Here rests
Ol' Dad

Gerald Chamberlain (1925-2003)
Willamette National Cemetery

I always knew they loved me
    — Yolanda

Otto & Martha Stoll
Oswego Pioneer Cemetery

I fold him close —
The child that's left to me.
My little lad who died.

Robert Garretson (1909-1911)
Oakwood Hill Cemetery

I miss my friend.

Manuel Rodriguez (1946-2003)
Coos River Cemetery

I stand here with a broken heart
I don't understand why you had to depart
Months pass by and still I grieve.
It's almost unbearable sometimes.
I believe some how [sic] I have to show my devotion
That my love for Anita is as deep as the ocean.
So I carve these words into stone to
Prove the love that I have shown

222

For my only daughter, and
Maybe she'll hear it possibly
Through some kind of spirit

Anon
Sunnyside Memorial

If we had a day to give
We'd surely give it to you
Just to hold you both once
to tell you we love you
and for you both
to know that we do.
  Love, Mom and Dad

Michael & David Gedlick (1987-1987)
Fairview-Scappoose Cemetery

In memory of my beloved wife into whose
dying eyes, upon whose death laid form I
I never glazed, and my child whom I never
saw in the grave with its mother.
My soul to God, my heart to you!

Abbie Boudreau (1896-1917)
Lewis and Clark Cemetery

In memory of
Thomas Herbert
Depated this life
Apr. 17, 1874
Aged
42 years
surounded by his afflicted
wife, Genvieve, and sorrowful
relatives.

Thomas Herbert (1832-1874)
Saint Paul's Cemetery (Saint Paul)

It'll be OK

No it won't.

Austin Lindquist (1991-1998)
Claggett Cemetery

Josie, Josie, I can't wait to see you
I can't wait to be with you
I can't wait to sit next to you
I can't wait to be in heaven with you

A song
  Your son Jack

> Josie Cohen (1953-1998)
> Lone Fir Cemetery

Just in the morning of his day
In youth and love he died

> William Holcomb (1888-1912)
> Eagle Valley Cemetery

Killed by a runaway team

> David Martin (1861-1893)
> Kelly Cemetery

Killed in action
Apr. 15, 1918

> Thomas Atchison (1887-1918)
> Mayger-Downing Community Church Cemetery

Last flight of "The Fox"

> Rodney Hallock (1964-1991)
> North Palestine Cemetery

Left at sea - we love you

> Johnny Gatens (1967-1995)
> Fern Ridge Cemetery (Seal Rock)

Lenny's little corner

> Arlen "Lenny" Shepherd (1958-1978)
> Bethany Pioneer Cemetery (Silverton)

Let her rest, let her sleep
Where the lone willow weeps.

I realize it's a palliative, but it it has a twilight sadness that appeals to me. I can see Alan Ladd standing over her grave.

Charity Harris (1866-1892)
Shadybrook Cemetery

Liam Joseph my little guy,
In the Lords [sic] arms now you
will lie.
I'm going to miss you so much
my son,
But now your [sic] in heaven where
you can run.
I just want to hold and
squeeze you tight,
Because I know you wouldn't
put up a fight.
As time goes on I want you
more.
Because caring for you was
never a chore.
Dont [sic] you worry, don't you fret,
Because your [sic] the one thing I
won't forget.
I love you Liam, my little man
I'll never forget you, no one can.
    Love
        Dad

Liam Shannon (1999-2003)
Hargadine Cemetery

Life so fragile,
Loss so sudden,
Heart so broken.

Timothy Bork (1964-2007)
Antioch Cemetery

Life's burden became
Too much to bear.
We understand, Ed.

Edwin Miller (1942-1973)
Cliffside Cemetery

225

Like doves do fly & eagles roar
That's me on my skateboard

> Cole
> River View Cemetery

Lord, we give unto you our little hero
Until the day that our arms may meet again

> Justyn Maes (1988-1995)
> Hubbard Cemetery

Loved husband
dad and grandpa
You know that

> Cleo Statham (1933-2007)
> Eagle Point National Cemetery

May there
Always be sounds of life

> Welch (1980-1980)
> Womer Cemetery

Mom and Dads [sic] Letter To
Our Angel Up In Heaven

As we lay in bed trying to rest our heads, we are starting
to question everything we do, in hope that maybe there
was a way we could have saved you.
In Mommy's arms we invited you to stay...
We had no idea that today would be the day in Daddy's
arms God would take you away.
We experienced today in no uncertain way how much you
were cared for.
As we look around and see all the friends you have found,
it's hard to believe you couldn't even speak to them.
Not even a sad last cry or whimper good-bye did we re-
ceive from you... I think in the end we will need to look
forward to when we will all be together again.
For now we need to remember what your sister said about
you.
Mommy, yesterday was our turn to play...

Now it is Gods [sic] turn today.
Please Lord Be With Our Son.

> Spencer Yanchik (1999-2000)
> Oak Hill Cemetery

Mother's only hope lies
buried here

> James Alva (1896-1918)
> Mount Zion Cemetery

Murdered by A. J. Weston

> Robert Krug (1849-1919)
> Camp Polk Cemetery

My baby's breath seems silent now,
'Til gentle breezes blow,
And then her voice comes quietly;
It whispers sweetly, then I know
Her perfect spirit lives and glows,
And I can feel her near.

> Janette Paolo (1984-1984)
> Yamhill-Carlton Cemetery

My daughter's life
was brief yet such
that in my emptiness
I have so much

> Esme Fuson (2003-2003)
> Lone Fir Cemetery (Portland)

My tears endless

> James Lyle (1921-2003)
> Willamette National Cemetery

No more pain
No more tears

> Fred Woods (1942-2005)
> Chief Schonchin Cemetery

No one's forgot

227

Forrest Erickson (1972-1994)
Gibbs Cemetery

Now I lay me down to sleep

Lisa Oxley (1961-1963)
Helvetia Cemetery
—
Patrick Wallace (1944-1944)
Mother Joseph Catholic Cemetery

On a beautiful Indian Summer day, 11/16/1976
in Sayre, PA, Andrew Gene Pack was born.
He grew into a fine young man, earning a masters
degree in physical therapy. He worked at
Legacy Medical Center in Gresham.
On 7/22/2005 in Ensenada, Mexico, four children
8 years old and younger were caught in a riptide
in the Pacific Ocean. Andy went in to help.
All the children survived. Andy did not.

Andrew Pack (1976-2005)
Forest Lawn Cemetery (Gresham)

Only God knows why.

Frederick Mink (1899-1937)
Union Cemetery (Union)

Our anchor in heaven

Cameron Prouty (1998-1998)
Elim Cemetery

Our brave little Codyman
Precious son

Cody Wood (1991-1992)
Bethany Pioneer Cemetery (Silverton)

Our dreams are sure gonna
   miss him

Glenn Daniels (2002-2002)
Finley Pioneer Cemetery

Our little artist in the sky

228

Isabella Martell (1994-1999)
Moehnke Cemetery

Our Man

J. J. White (1940-1942)
Robert Bird Cemetery

Our Mighty Quinn

*How do you explain a shooting star that shined so bright-
ly, touched so many lives and left so quickly...*

Quinn Mitchell (2001-2001)
Lone Fir Cemetery

Pearl Harbor Survivor

William Feight (1918-2001)
Willamette National Cemetery

Princess
Angel
Ballerina
Miracle Baby
Girl Friend
Dear Heart

Emily Stewart (1995-2003)
Columbia Memorial Cemetery

Remembering Kain

We see spiky hair
Playing with Raegan and she's laughing
Wall Ba; Champion
Hand up in the air
Kain's 2 front teeth are gone
Rolling his fruit snacks into a big ball
He had lots of Pride Prints
Learning finger knitting
We smell cookies he is serving
Sweat after PE and recess
Tart green apples for snack
We hear, "Ms. Yuchos can I read with you today?"

The Jingle Bell Song
Sounding out words
Kain pounding his chest playing King Kong
We feel happy when he played King Kong with us
Sad when we miss him
Happy when we remember his smile and laugh

June 2006

> Kain Phomphakdy (1998-2006)
> Forest Lawn (Gresham)

Rest in peace
Happy little camper

> Antonio Leonardo (1975-1989)
> Frank Abel

Rest, soldier, rest,
thy warfare o'er.

> Hermann Bruns (1845-1904)
> Firhill Cemetery

Running above the clouds

> Christopher Miller (1971-1987)
> Burns Cemetery

Saved Through the Prayers of Our Mother

> Jose Wilson (1862-1882) & Roland McDonald (1864-
> 1882)
> Lone Fir Cemetery (Portland)

She died a tragic death and was unclaimed. As long as a
stranger cares, she will always be remembered. She's in
God's care.

Anonymous victim of a serial killer.

> Jane Doe
> Adams Cemetery

She gave so much and asked for so little
[under her name]

He really tried
   [under his name]

> Ronald (b. 1939) & Marianne (1940-1995) Fultz
> Turner Twin Oaks Cemetery

She was spirited
Sixteen and ready for life.
A plane crash took her
In an instant.
May her soul be bound to everlasting life.

> Elana Gold (1975-1991)
> Beth Israel Cemetery

She was too good too gentle and fair
To dwell in this cold world of care

> Anon
> Unknown cemetery in Montana or Idaho.

Sheltered and safe
From sorrow.

> William Bagley (1852-1902)
> Paisley Cemetery

Sometime don't you think
It's wiser not to grow up

> Benjamin Craig (1974-1977)
> Saint Mary Cemetery (Enterprise, WA)

Sometimes God needs a bud or blossom to scatter with
   the full blooms in his garden, so he takes the rarest he
   can find

> Brian Lawyer (1981-2000)
> Union Cemetery (Union)

South Vietnam 1969-1975
Earth has no sorrow
That heaven cannot heal

> Daniel Lacy (1948-1989)
> Stearns Cemetery

231

Sweet angel of mine how dear you are to be by my side, to
*   take*
My soul from the sick ness [sic] of this world to the gates
*   of heaven*
To protect and love as you once did. For I cherished my
*   life on earth.*
Bless my family for I have left them in a world of sorrow.
*   [heart] Andrea*

> Beraldo Alegria (1947-1999)
> Arivaca Cemetery (Arizona)

T is for treasure, a heart of gold
A is for affectionate, a lovable soul
N is for natural, a gift from Above
A is for angel, precious and loved

> Tana Woodburn (1983-1996)
> Canyon Hill Cemetery

The child we had, but never had,
And yet will have Forever.

> Eric Lukkasson (2004-2004)
> Miller Cemetery (Scio)

The day the music died

> Carroll Simmon (1943-2005)
> Pleasant Valley Cemetery

The Geer twins

Conceived as one. Lived as two
Together forever

They died within three months of each other.

> Sally Klukkert (1941-2004) & Florence Macpherson
>   (1941-2004)
> IOOF Cemetery (Fossil)

The happiest and saddest day
of our lives; we'll see you
when we get there J. R.
*   Love, Mom & Dad*

James Oliphant III (2000-2000)
Coles Valley Cemetery

The measure of a life is not the
Duration but the donation

Gary (1986-1988) & Frederick (1986-1987) Hussey
Drewsey Cemetery

The price of freedom is written on the wall

This is written at the peak (highest point) of the Vietnam Memorial. It may be an exalted interpretation of those events.

Larry Beck (1944-2000)
Howell Cemetery

The tortured mind
and the anguished soul are at rest.

Raymond DeFord (1981-2006)
Rainier Cemetery (WA)

There is a bridge
'Tween here and there
Beyond the sky above
A path of communication
Made up of our love

Sweet child of mine —
Though forever young, you had maturity
In spirit and in soul —
You're the inspiration, for eternity
Love you Kelly

Anon
La Center Cemetery

Thirteen once composed our number,
Father, mother, sisters, brothers.
Ah, well! for us all some sweet hope lies
Deeply buried from human eyes.

Anon
Turner Twin Oaks Cemetery

This is where the cowboy rides away

If there's one classic Western epitaph, this is it.

Juston Teel (1972-1999)
Weston Cemetery

This little hand
will never grow.
It will always
stay just so.
And when I'm big
and far away
This little hand
will with you stay.

This poem shows up anonymously on a British parenting site, but its origins are obscure.

Jimmy Bishop (1993-1997)
Eugene Masonic Cemetery

This Taylor made life was the perfect fit
For the girl who could never sit.
She would be the first one to greet you at the door
And the last one to see you go
And sometimes she would even try to follow you home.
Whether she wore a frown from disgust
Or a smile of mirth
She was always the most gorgeous child to walk the
    earth.
So for the little lady everybody loved
There's no need to mourn her
Because she's dancing in the clouds above.

Taylor Overton (1999-2002)
Crescent Grove Cemetery

Time was so short
But I loved you
Time was so short
Too short to know you
Enough time will never go by
To forget you

Michael Moffat (1979-1979)

234

To you from me
Mark,
You were the littlest of all,
but not very small.
Your smile was bright,
It stood out like a light.
Your eyes they were blue,
Like a deep dark pool.
You were one of a kind,
And never behind.
Your were in a class of your
Own and never alone.
You lost your life,
By being free
You were someone
I could not be.
"But"
As the hurt goes away,
The emptiness is here to stay.
I just want to say,
In my very own way,
I love you,
Always and forever.
Jeannette

> Mark DeClue (1965-1982)
> Tygh Valley Cemetery

Too beautiful to exist
In this life.

> Mariah Wieberdink (1973-1973)
> Columbian Cemetery

Troubled soul rest in peace

> R. S. Shook (1828-1884)
> Noble Pioneer Cemetery

Two little rosebuds

> Beulah (1918-1918) & Ruth (1920-1926) Matthes
> Hayesville Cemetery

Watching over you

> Joseph Pinkston (1913-2003)
> Willamette National Cemetery

Watching your back

> Wray Humbyrd (1941-2003)
> Willamette National Cemetery

We hope you had the time of your life

[verso]

There are no words for love and pain so deep.
He was ours to borrow not to keep.
So many hopes, so much joy
Are here with our wonder boy.

> Tyler Walker (1993-2006)
> Woodville Cemetery

We love you to the moon and back.

> Adam Williams (2000-2000)
> Saint Francis Catholic Cemetery

We miss you, Ladybug

> Melinda Mulder (1974-1994)
> Mountain View Corbett Pioneer Cemetery

We will always love you because
you are our little bug-a-boo

> Cody Garth (1989-1990)
> Washougal Memorial Cemetery

Whose plane was lost off
Santo Domingo and
was never found

> Gerold Goff (1937-1971)
> Pleasant Hill Cemetery (Pleasant Hill)

You have found that

Long highway home

Ronald Gilbert Sr (1951-2002)
Willamette National Cemetery

You went to sleep knowing
that we love you. That is
the most precious gift of all.
God has a special place in
his heart for little boys.

We'll love you forever,
Littleman
  Mom, Dad, Kate & Emma

Bailey Schlentz (1999-2006)
La Center Cemetery

You'll hunt with us always

Alby Brundidge (1981-2002)
Aumsville Cemetery

Love Me Do
(Romantics)

For the most part, these romantic epitaphs are modern; as a consequence they're ordered alphabetically. It's certainly possible that I've put epitaphs here that belong among the quotes—I presume you'll tell me—I couldn't have caught them all. It's hard to read them and not feel the arc of intersecting lives. So many times one is looking at youth through the eyes of death. There is a more reassuring poignancy here, though, than among the epitaphs for children. Lovers looking closely can still see the fading light of their partners. Somewhere lurks the epitaph, "Red skies tonight/ Sailor's delight."

❖

A family's heart

> Ronald Plahn (1931-2002)
> Yankton Community Fellowship Cemetery

A light that shines on

> Samantha Hopper (1988-2005)
> Restlawn Cemetery

A mountain to climb to her smile divine

> Wayne (b. 1939) & Mary Jane (1941-1996) Stavang
> Pioneer Cemetery (Jordan)

A rainbow of color
My easel of life

> Maryida Millsap (b. 1922)
> Alford Cemetery

Amidst the thorns
Came God's fragile flower
And now a bouquet adorns

> Marietta Cunningham (1933-1978)
> Eureka Cemetery

As they walk hand in hand
Through the gateway to heaven
May they rest in peace forever

> Betty (1946-1988) & Roy (1949-1988) Meier
> Evergreen Memorial Cemetery

At rest on the prairie they loved so dear

> Helen (1921-2007) & James (1917-2002) Silcox
> Forks Cemetery

Bob carried Dodie's book to h.s.

> Dodie & Bob Greer
> Lone Fir Cemetery (Portland)

Butterfly kisses forever, Daddy.

Arthur rose again from myth - superimposed over historical figures and legendary heroes. His legacy is the persistence of his ideals. His story does not fade away.

How lucky we are, for all too short a time, to live in Camelot, led by this man whose arms were large enough to encompass us all. How blessed we are that he planted his heart so deeply within our own that, as long as we live, he will live too, for we will dare yet to dream. - Cherie

I will love you forever, Sweetheart

> Lee Ertsgaard (1962-2002)
> City View Cemetery

Earth's brightest gems are fading.

> Pearl Archer
> Saint Mary's Cemetery (Hood River)

Eternity blossoms for her
with stars

> Sydney Moffit (1943-2003)
> Eugene Masonic Cemetery

Eyes so dark and dear

> Eugene (1909-2001) & Anne (1908-2002) Petuchov
> Springwater Cemetery

From my remains shall grow a tall and sturdy tree. And alongside from yours a beautiful flower. We shall nod and

smile and whisper in the breezes to one another, and greet
our friends as they pass through the meadow.

Donald (1916-1996) & Dorothy (1913-1983) Kyle
Gales Creek Cemetery

Gentle abloom skin   Elegant decorous inner shell   Deli-
cate
tender smile seen by the blind   Cosmic flower engraved in
a bowl
of earth Without one another, sorrowful existence   Wash
the
fright away with one hand   The other leads us through
the
undaunted luminous shadows of love   With true un-
bounded devotion

Gonzales
Municipal/Lakeview Cemeteries (Galveston, TX)

Hand in hand across the years I have walked with you.
In deep green forests - on desert sand.
And now our time on earth is through, in heaven too, we'll
hold hands.

Paul (1917-2006) & Rebecca (b. 1920) Kidwell
Redmond Memorial Cemetery

Have I told you lately I love you

Nancy (1932-1992) & Jim (b. 1928) Hall
Enterprise Cemetery

He arrived with the snow
He left with the wind
someday
we'll be together again

Richard Banker (1968-1995)
West Lawn Cemetery

He had the sweetest brown eyes
And a smile to light up the world

Kyle Holland (1982-2003)
Greenwood Cemetery (Cathlamet)

241

He is just a memory away

Steven Bonny (1967-1993)
Mountain View Memorial

He led diamonds
She returned hearts

A.C.B.L. Life Masters

Anon
Lower Boise Cemetery

Here lies love—
Sweetly sleeping. Bear this in mind
Those of you whose paths have, here, entwined
A more loving mother, there's never been,
Nor a better wife or truer friend.
Begin with laughter, end the same
In reverie while you speak her name...
Remember her smile, her faith, her cheer
Kneel not in sorrow, nor grieve, while here
But plant a kiss upon the Earth
To prove and acknowledge you knew her worth.
With mirth recall memories you're most fond of,
But, pray, tread softly, for here lies love.

Connie Silvestri (1951-2005)
Evergreen Cemetery (Seaside)

Hey Darlin'

Lillian Engel (1915-2005)
Havurah Shalom Cemetery

I am always here to understand you.
I am always here to laugh with you.
I am always here to cry with you.
I am always here to talk to you.
Even though we might not always be
Together, please know that I am
Always here to love you.

Scott Geving (1971-1990)

I am with you always
To the very end of the age

> Sharon (1948-2005) & Wesley (b. 1946) Wood
> Alford Cemetery

"...how we would make the kisses fly."

> Ira Goodell 1873-1894
> Lone Fir Cemetery (Portland)

The early date on this is remarkable. Twenty-one and in love.

I know I loved you before I knew you
and today I love you more than ever
We thank God for blessing us with you

> Richie Landaverde
> Cornelius United Methodist Cemetery

I love you—all of you
Whether you can see me or not
I still love you - CLA

> Christi Abbey (1952-1986)
> Orting Cemetery

I love you in a place
that has no space or time.
I love you for my life,
you are a friend of mine.
Always and forever.

> Robert Strassburg (1943-1998)
> Pleasant Hill Cemetery (Pleasant Hill)

I love you more today than yesterday
But not as much as tomorrow

> Merle (1944-2001) & Vickie (b. 1946) Clemens
> Westside Cemetery

I love you not only for what you are but for what I am
when I'm with you.

Patricia (1945-2004) & Floyd (b. 1943) Robinson
Valley View Cemetery

I love you to your toes

Shirley & James (1946-2005) Sauerwein
Mount Calvary Catholic Cemetery

I walked with you once upon a dream

Erten Brock (1939-2005)
Walker Community Church

I won't be far away, for life goes on.
Just listen to your heart and you will hear
All my love around you.

Travis Moser (1981-2000)
Old Carson Cemetery

If the angels have sweethearts, I still want you for mine.

Lois (1929-1995) & Lee (1919-1989) Kelly
Gilliland Cemetery

If I could choose again
I'd choose you

Carole Blair (1944-1996)
Waitsburg Cemetery

I'll find my way back to you by heart.

Darlene Urban (1966-2007)
Saint John Lutheran/Salmon Creek Pioneer Cemetery

I'll meet you in the morning

Marion Northup (1917-1996)
Shadybrook Cemetery

Junipers and roses - forever

Charles (1930-2000) & Jan (b. 1943) Crawford
IOOF Cemetery (Fossil)

Left our hearts in Budapest

Anna (1944-2002) & Karoly (b. 1935) Koczian
Mount Calvary Catholic Cemetery

Let me sleep
in the arms of your nightfall,
Let me laugh
in the sunlight of your smile,
Let me run
on the edge of forever.
Let me stay
forever in the warmth of your love

Rachel (b. 1941) & Ernest (1939-2005) Smith
Columbia Memorial Cemetery

Like a bird in flight I send you this dove
To deliver this message of my undying love

John West (1947-1978)
Reedsport Masonic Cemetery

Listen as I sing "I love you"

Robert Pilgreen (1963-1991)
Miller Cemetery

Look for me; I'll be there too

Martha & Thomas
Lone Oak Cemetery

Love you more

Last word written edgewise.

Ernestine Duhrkoop (1929-2002)
Lone Fir Cemetery (Portland)

Love you softly
Forever   Tim

Ropp
Normal Hill Cemetery

Made my dreams
Come true

Fred Parker (1933-2003)

Meet me in
That city
Where the roses never fade

> Edna (1914-1982) & Floyd (1912-1997) Landis
> Adams Cemetery

Memories as beautiful as roses.

> Babe Fitzharris (1912-1975)
> Tualatin Plains Presbyterian Church Cemetery

Mi Maruja,
Mi vida empezó el diá que nos casamos
Ahora esta perdido porque tu no estas
No hay consuelo para mi dolor
Asi yo, tambien, tendre que morir
para encontrar alivio.
> *Con todo mi amor,*
> *Daniel*

My Maruja,
My life began the day we got married
Now it's lost because you are no more
There's no consolation for my sadness
Such that I too would have to die
to receive relief
  With all my love
  Daniel

> Doña Mariá Palús de Carroll (1935-1990)
> Saint Johns Catholic Cemetery (Barberton)

My wife til the end of time

> Debbie (1954-1994) & Eddie (b. 1939) Hogan
> Fern Prairie Cemetery

Nothing perfect lasts forever
except in our memories

> Billie Thomas (1927-2003) & Darlene (b. 1942)
> Livermore
> IOOF Cemetery (Fossil)

Now she can see Mt. Hood forever

Indeed, Mountain View Corbett has an unparalleled close-up view of Portland's Mt. Fuji, sometimes known by its native name, Wy'east.

Thelma Johnson (1929-1989)
Mountain View Corbett Pioneer Cemetery

Now she has her rainbow & roses

Cheri Androscheck (1958-2002)
Lone Fir Cemetery (Portland)

Our golden daybreak

Vernon (1915-2000) & Vivian (b. 1920) Embley
Bunker Hill Cemetery

Our highway
Will never end

David & Barbara Heffner (1952-2002)
Willamette National Cemetery

Our Last Flight

Robert (b. 1901) & Iris (1988-1906)
Estacada IOOF Cemetery

Our lives were touched
because we walked a special walk together
because we mattered to each other
because we were friends
because we gave each other courage
because we cared
because we loved each other.

Lawrence McLaren (1922-2002)
Lewisville Cemetery

Our love and memories last forever—
His smile, his laugh, his kind heart,
His arm waving from the Chevy window

Rohs Kuppinger (1983-2001)
Joseph Cemetery

Remember each day,
right from the start,

247

I will be forever near,
for I live within your hearts.

> Travis Davis (1965-2006)
> Carus Cemetery

Remember that I
Love you so much

> Richard & Patricia (1940-2000) Lawyer
> Willamette National Cemetery

Remember us
Who we were
Before time took us away
The life we shared
The way we laughed and
Loved on those endless days

Remember us
We were much in love
We smiled and laughed thru our days
We shared a life
We joined our hearts
We now dance the Milky Way

> Joseph (b. 1950) & Nancy (1950-2002) Evans
> Springfield Memorial Gardens

Searching for Linda
on the Oregon Trail

> Nathan Hand
> Lyle-Balch Cemetery

Serenity

The quiet strength of shadowed hills
the timeless patience of the pine
the solace of the constant sea
and your hand holding mine
Sassy to Ray, 1963

> Lola Middaugh (b. 1939)
> Yachats Memorial Park

248

She brought magic to ordinary days

> Debra Allis (1956-2004)
> Spring Valley Presbyterian Cemetery

She walked softly and stole our hearts

> Betty Slavin (1951-2008)
> Laurel Cemetery

She was — but words are
wanting to say what.
Think what a wife should
be, she was that.

> S. A. Conrad (1836-1882)
> Odd Fellows Cemetery (Myrtle Creek)

She was his rose; he was her wall
Together, forever, in the garden

> Sadie (1915-1997) & Haven (1914-1997) Benson
> Joseph Cemetery

Sleep, Love, until we meet again.

> Lucretia Eones (1861-1896)
> Clatsop Plains Pioneer Cemetery

So little time
So many lovely memories

> Darell & Betty
> Evergreen Memorial Cemetery

Some of our most joyful, fulfilling, happy, trusting and
serene years have been spent together. We will always
love each other.

> Ralph (1928-2001) & Susan (b. 1938) Hanley
> Spring Valley Presbyterian Church Cemetery

The ripples of her love echo far beyond anything we might
say

> Edgar (b. 1923) & Lillie (1925-1991) May
> Dallas Cemetery

The rose
She was plucked before her time

> JoAnn DeLaRosa (1955-2000)
> Bethany Pioneer Cemetery (Silverton)

The mountain looks so beautiful...
The mist is swirling around it.
The sun is setting behind it.
The mountain looks so beautiful...
Everything is so still. Except me.
I am looking at the mountain
Because that's where I'll be
*   when you reach me.*
The mountain looks so beautiful...
I'm here.
*   Teryn Leigh*

> James Shultz (1984-2000)
> Star #23 Rebekah Lodge Cemetery

They planted trees together

> Harold (1916-1993) & Valerie (1915-2003) Nelson
> Bonanza Cemetery

They shared a love for learning
Natural science, and each other.

> John (1945-1994) & Beckianne (b. 1945) Kilkenny
> Saint Joseph Catholic Cemetery (Roseburg)

Twas her thinking of others
Makes you think of her

> Margaret Emerick (1955-2002)
> Greenwood Cemetery (Cathlamet)

Unconditional love given
Unconditional love received

> Wm. Holderman (1949-1990)
> Jones Pioneer Cemetery

We love you a bushel
And a peck and a peck

Around the neck

> Constance Olds (1917-2000)
> Lone Fir Cemetery

We were in this together

> Esther Knight (1991-2008)
> Pilot Butte / Greenwood Cemetery

What an imprint your footsteps
Have left upon our heart

> Sé White (d. 2000)
> Smith Cemetery

What the heart has once known, it shall never lose.

> Scott Bland (1959-1983)
> River View Cemetery

When a lovely
Flame dies

> R. Alan Resleure (1923-2000)
> Willamette National Cemetery

When I close my eyes I see your face
But all these tears will never
Erase the face, the smile or the
Million good times we dwell on
Our love is eternal

> Aaron Milton (1976-1994)
> Washougal Memorial Cemetery

wild & crazy kids

> Glen (1931-2006) & Geraldine (1933-1994) Pearson
> Roseburg National Cemetery

within this paper deep in its fold there lies
my hand for you to hold. It will always be
there and never fade Because it
was filled with love when
it was made when you lay
your hand upon mine and

251

gave it that touch always
remember these words
it means just as much

> Richard Huss (1973-1999)
> La Center Cemetery

You may be one person to the world
But to one person you are the world.

Yes, it's a palliative, but I thought I'd give Judy the benefit of the doubt.

> Judy Bunch (1938-2007)
> Bunker Hill Cemetery

Your love is like the wind,
I can't see it but I can feel it.

> Jimmy Gonzales (1964-2003)
> Multnomah Park Pioneer Cemetery

GRAB BAG, TAG END, FIRE SALE

Maybe they could have been put somewhere else, but each of them lives slightly by itself. There are only a handful. Make of them what you will. They are arranged alphabetically.

An idealist and a dreamer. He died of loneliness and
a broken heart, searching for a shrine he never found.

[Followed by the name and dates of his dog, Lady Gwi-
  navier, who he characterized as "A loyal and faithful
  friend./ She believed in the dream."]

It's been said that man is the most evolved of
all animals on this planet, or is he? I know
of no other living creature that perverts
what he knows and destroys what he does not.

[verso]

A parting note for those who pass by.
If you quest for the line between truth
and reality, you'll find it in the "Hs" under
honor, in the library of ambivalence.
        Sterling Drake
        12-25-1998

There is no way to do justice to Mr. Drake's pre-deceased marker without visuals. I'll try. It's in the shape of a large—three or more feet—black granite X, six or eight inches thick. One side is emblazoned a sword crossed with a rocket over the two strokes of the X. On the reverse an embryo occupies the center of the X with an umbilical cord heading out one arm towards God knows what, while the other arms carry a hand holding a key, a strand of DNA, and a mushroom-shaped cloud and the formula $E=mc^2$. There's more. I'll stop.

    Mr. Drake is still with us. A documentary has been made about this stone, which I have not seen. It is a disturbing stone.

                Sterling Drake (b. 1945)
                Mountain View Cemetery (Walla Walla)

Dedicated in filial love
To the memory of
My Dear Mother

Babette
Consort of
Jacob Oppenheimer.

> Babette Oppenheimer (1828-1893)
> Beth Israel Cemetery

Give me freedom, not peace   For I am a free man

Pardon the editorial comment, but are those antithetical?

> Charles Campbell Jr. (1956-1998)
> Lookingglass Cemetery

He was there when we needed him

> Harold Brazille (1927-1962)
> Pleasant Valley Cemetery

Just you & me, simple & free

> Ted Church (1955-1997)
> Ilwaco Cemetery

Lord God, our
power evermore,
Whose arm doth
reach the ocean
floor,
Dive with our men
beneath the sea,
Traverse the
depths
protectively,
O hear us when we
pray, and keep
them safe from
peril in the deep.

> Robert (b. 1941) & Marjorie (1945-2007) Biersner
> Mountain View Cemetery (Walla Walla)

Tak for alt

"Thanks for everything"; traditional Norwegian epitaph.

> Emma (b. 1920)

254

Thank you for the
Gift of curiosity
    Love Carlene

> Carl Anderson (1907-2004)
> Roseburg National Cemetery

Write me as one who loves his fellow man

> Benjamin Cornelius (1834-1881)
> Mountain View Memorial Cemetery

INDEX

First lines are in *italics*; names are in **bold**.

First lines are as they appear on the monument. The order of names, where there are multiples, is as they appear on the monument, left to right when facing the monument. There are two schools of thought on alphabetising: either by first word first, second word second, and so on; or strict alphabetisation without regard to words. The program with which this book was laidout, Adobe's InDesign, was of the latter school.

Numbers

A

258

261

D

269

271

273

L

281

282

284

289

S

293

U

V

W

299

Z

DEAD SPACE

There are slightly over 400 cemeteries in this list, most from Oregon, with lesser amounts from Washington and Idaho, plus a few from other places (like Texas) because they were there. My greater interest is in what's written on tombstones rather than from where they're from; although all but a handful are from the Oregon Territory. I stopped before including directions for the cemeteries; that would have entailed an enormous book. Instead, you can find them on my Flickr site, DEADMANTALKING (**http://www.flickr.com/photos/deadmantalking/**). There are another 400-plus cemeteries at that site, along with some 17,000 photographs.

A

B

P

315

318

34108155R00184

Made in the USA
San Bernardino, CA
19 May 2016